TALES OF THE UNEXPECTED

TALES OF THE UNEXPECTED

THE
DAVE
BEASANT
S T O R Y

DAVE BEASANT
W I T H
DAVE SMITH

MAINSTREAM
PUBLISHING

First published in Great Britain in 1989 by
MAINSTREAM PUBLISHING COMPANY (EDINBURGH) LTD
7 Albany Street, Edinburgh EH1 3UG

ISBN 1 85158 220 7 (cloth)

British Library Cataloguing in Publication Data
Beasant, Dave
   Tales of the unexpected.
   1. England. Association Football. Beasant, Dave
   I. Title   II. Smith, Dave
   796.334′092′4

ISBN 1-85158-220-7

Typeset in 11½pt Imprint by Bookworm Typesetting Ltd., Edinburgh.
Printed in Great Britain by Billing and Sons Ltd., Worcester.

CONTENTS

Foreword

by

Dave Bassett

I have known and respected Dave Beasant for many years and if anyone deserved to reap the fruits of success that the game of football reserves for special people it's the fella we know affectionately as 'Lurch'. In the years we worked together at Wimbledon I always regarded him as the perfect professional – and a terrific captain too. He's got a very sensible head on those broad shoulders and it was vital to me, and Wimbledon FC, to have a player with so many excellent qualities as my skipper and right-hand man. Unlike some players who might argue the toss with their manager over certain things Dave was always able to communicate in a proper, professional manner. He was my voice to the rest of the players, the ideal middle-man who could put my opinions across to the lads and similarly relay their thoughts or grievances to me. I will always have the utmost respect for him for that reason.

He has also proved himself to be a tremendous goalkeeper with the temperament and consistency to be a success at any club, at any level. Mind you, there was a time when I was assistant manager at Wimbledon that I feared I had dropped an almighty clanger in persuading the then boss Dario Gradi to give this gangly youth from Edgware Town (a 'rank amateur' as I called him at the time) a chance at Plough Lane. Dario had his doubts about Dave from day one, especially when he saw him turn up for work on his motorbike, and Lurch's disastrous home debut did nothing to convince Dario I'd unearthed a goalkeeping gem. Far from it in fact. After Dave let Blackpool's winning goal through his legs in his first game I was told, in no uncertain terms, to find another 'keeper. I had been pushing for Dave to be put in the team and I took some stick from Dario as a result. But thankfully, for Dave and the club, we kept faith with him and he went on to become a first-class 'keeper and a great ambassador for Wimbledon generally.

Once he'd put his debut behind him I knew he would go all the way to the top and I'm delighted he's gone on to achieve so much in the game. He may have thought at times that fame and fortune had passed him by but he kept plugging away and has now reaped the rewards. His finest hour came in the 1988 FA Cup Final when he first saved a penalty from John Aldridge (as I knew he would) and then, as captain, went to collect the famous trophy. I was at Wembley that day and seeing him hold the FA Cup aloft from the Royal box made me feel very proud. Of course, there were pangs of regret on my part, having left the club a year before, but my feelings were dominated by ones of sheer delight for a great bunch of lads.

I was equally pleased when, soon after that Wembley triumph, Dave got the big money transfer to Newcastle that no one could have denied him. He'd been a tremendous servant for Wimbledon but the time was right to move on and sample life on the other side of the fence. It would have been wrong for him to stay at Plough Lane for the rest of his career because he needed, and deserved, to play for a big club. As was the case for me at my first club after Wimbledon – Watford – things didn't go so well for Dave at Newcastle but in true Wimbledon style he's bounced back with Chelsea and now the world is his oyster. Being such a super-fit athlete Dave could, like Peter Shilton, go on playing at the top for another ten years. And, having forced his way into the England reckoning, a full international cap is now well within his reach. No one deserves one more.

CHAPTER ONE

Beyond My Wildest Dreams

As I stood facing Princess Diana with the FA Cup gleaming between us it all seemed too good to be true. I kept thinking that I would wake up at any second to discover that it had all been an incredible dream. It wasn't. I'd fantasised about this moment a hundred times but now it was for real – Wimbledon had won the Cup and I was about to receive the coveted trophy from a true-to-life Princess.

I can't really remember what I said to her, if I managed to say anything at all, because my head was spinning with excitement and emotion. I remembered the great skippers of the past standing in almost the same spot – people like Bryan Robson, Alan Hansen, Kevin Ratcliffe and Steve Perryman. Suddenly it was my turn to savour the moment and join the stars in the history books as the latest captain of a Cup-winning team. I just wanted to take hold of the trophy and show it to our supporters gathered on the right hand side of this magnificent stadium. Wembley had never looked so beautiful. The roar which greeted my raising of the FA Cup bedecked in blue and yellow ribbons may not have been as thunderous as in the past but to me it said everything; Wimbledon had achieved the impossible. The paupers of London had beaten Liverpool, the princes of Merseyside, and there couldn't have been a dry Wimbledon eye in the house.

It was the moment we'd all dreamed of and the moment millions of cynics had said would never happen. Some even suggested we weren't fit to grace such an occasion but by now they were all eating enormous pieces of humble pie while we savoured the icing on the cake. 'Wimbledon haven't got a hope,' they said; 'Wimbledon: they play tennis, don't they?' they asked; 'There's only one team in it,' they ventured. We proved them all wrong and the remarkable success story no one wanted written was there for everyone to read every time they picked up a soccer history book. From Southern League giant killers to FA Cup winners in little more than ten glorious years – that was the magnitude of Wimbledon's achievement. No one could take it away from us.

It was also a measure of my own personal accomplishment – from non-League obscurity with Edgware Town to Wembley glory. The lad whose home overlooked the most celebrated football stadium in the world was now a Cup final hero –

Face to Face with a real life Princess.

in more ways than one. I had become the first goalkeeper to lead a team out of the famous tunnel for an FA Cup final; the first to lift the trophy on such an occasion; and the first to save a penalty in the process. I even picked up the 'Man of the Match' award just for good measure. I have never been as proud as I was holding the trophy aloft that afternoon and I will treasure the memories as long as I live. If I could have sat down and written the script beforehand it wouldn't have done justice to the remarkable sequence of events which transpired. It all seemed too good to be true and the champagne celebrations which followed back at the considerably more humble surroundings of Plough Lane provided the perfect end to what had been a perfect day.

The build-up to Wimbledon's greatest day, however, began long before that glorious afternoon of 14 May 1988. In fact straight after the semi-final victory over Luton more than a month before plans were being laid to ensure that, whatever the outcome, we would make it a day to remember. 'After all, we may never get to Wembley again.' From the moment we beat Luton EVERYTHING was geared to the Cup final and even the League took second place. We won only one First Division match on the run-in to Wembley (even before the semis our League form wasn't too clever) and it wasn't difficult to see where our attention lay. But can you blame us? In our last game before the final – against Manchester United – we were all conscious of the fact that one bad knock could put us out of the big match and I can honestly say that was the only time I can ever remember a Wimbledon side failing to match the opposition in a battle. After we'd gone 1-0 up United suddenly turned nasty, feet were flying and studs were showing which was the last thing we wanted just five days before the Cup final. United eventually came back to win 2-1 and, while everyone knows that Wimbledon love a good scrap, on this occasion United took advantage of our situation and we didn't want to know. I suppose people will say we 'bottled it' on the day but we were simply protecting ourselves for the Saturday. On another day we could have made it quite interesting. The important thing was that we all came through unscathed and manager Bobby Gould was able to name his strongest team for Wembley.

Before the big day, however, there were a million and one things for us to do; attend functions; stage Press conferences and photo-sessions; make TV appearances; make a Cup final record at the famous Abbey Road studios; you name it, we did it. We even became fashion models for a day, starring in the TV programme *The Clothes Show* parading our Wembley suits and other gear provided by Top Shop. But it wasn't just the players who were involved in the events leading up to the final. Wives, girlfriends, children, even the office staff were all made to feel part of this great occasion and that was typical of the family spirit on which the club had thrived over the years. Without it we wouldn't have got to Wembley at all. It was good being involved in so many things during the build-up because it helped take our minds off the big day and it wasn't until the Friday before the game that the tension began to mount. That was when Bobby Gould pulled a master stroke.

At about nine p.m. as we sat around our hotel digesting our evening meal – and chewing nervously over the events which were to follow – Alan Cork, the 'old man' of the side chirped up: 'What are we going to do now boss, go down the pub?' He said it in jest, at least I think he did, but Bob considered it a good idea and told us to go out and enjoy ourselves. Going out for a drink the night before a game was something we had been accustomed to at Wimbledon and, even though it was the eve of the biggest day in our lives, the boss saw no need to break with tradition. In fact he was genuinely keen on the idea, feeling it would do us good to go out and relax, although with his blessing came a few words of warning – 'don't go mad and don't be late back'. So with that we got up, walked out of the hotel and headed for the nearest pub.

It was a funny situation, and probably one only Wimbledon could find themselves in, but in my mind it was a shrewd move by the boss which arguably paid dividends on the day itself. The pub we visited was only a few hundred yards away from the hotel and inside the supporters were preparing for the final in their own way. You should have seen the look on their faces when the people they would be cheering on in less than 18 hours' time walked in to join them at the bar. You could have heard a pin drop. To us it was nothing unusual but the fans couldn't believe it was happening on the eve of the Cup final. But that was Wimbledon for you; unpredictable to the end. I've never been averse to the odd half of Guinness before a game and that's what I ordered, with Corky indulging in a lager along with one or two of the other lads. Those who didn't normally drink made do with a fruit juice.

We spent about an hour or so relaxing in the pub talking to the fans about the game and generally having a good time. We discovered a few things that we never knew about Wimbledon FC too. We learned that, in the days when Wimbledon played their games on the Common nearby, the club used that very same pub as their changing room. Call it fate if you like. We also met a terrific old guy in his eighties who had been following Wimbledon since he was a kid, so the evening turned into quite a nostalgic occasion. But, as the boss requested, we didn't go mad with the drink and by about ten thirty we were back in the hotel none the worse for wear. In fact we were in a far better state of mind than we would have been lounging around the hotel thinking about the game – and it showed in our relaxed attitude the following morning. I think we all slept well (I know I did) and when the big day arrived there were no signs of nerves in the camp at all as we soaked up the sun on the hotel patio. Everyone was so relaxed that you wouldn't have believed we were on the brink of creating club history and at one point I remember looking at Corky strolling around with his Ray-bans on and wondering whether we were TOO laid back. But really, we were just hell-bent on savouring every moment of a day that might not come again.

One of the first things we did after breakfast was scour the newspapers to see what our journalistic 'friends' had written about us – and they didn't let us down. Almost every paper had written us off before a ball was kicked and one even suggested that it would be disastrous for the game in this country if we won. 'For the good of football Liverpool must win', they said. All the so-called experts succeeded in doing, however, was to fire us up even more and make us doubly determined to ram the words so far down their throats they would choke. The few writers who did give us a chance were made out to be idiots who were ready for the strait-jacket. But it didn't really matter to us what people were writing because we were confident in our own minds that we could turn Liverpool over. Being the underdogs in what was supposed to be 'the most one-sided Cup final of all time' we had nothing to lose.

Just before we left the hotel my wife, Sandra, together with the other players' wives and girlfriends, all kitted out with their new dresses, came along to see us off with a kiss and a smile and they looked almost as good as we did in our new suits! With a yellow rose and blue ribbon providing the finishing touch we looked a million dollars. Everyone was in great humour. We were determined to enjoy our day whatever the outcome and it was with that attitude that we climbed aboard the coach and set off for Wembley. We certainly travelled in style on a luxury coach – complete with TV crew – although the Press had been speculating as to whether we would arrive at Wembley in the old mini-bus as Bob had done at White Hart Lane, Tottenham, for the semis. In an interview with Martin Tyler for *The Saint and Greavsie* show I even suggested that, as I lived so close to Wembley, I would probably walk to the game. A joke of course. There was no way I was going to miss that coach ride down Wembley Way. It's as much a part of the day as the game itself. As it turned out, the route we took to Wembley was pretty much the same as I'd used almost every day for the past ten years to get to and from the training ground. Every day as I passed Wembley I'd cast a glance at the famous twin towers and wonder. Well now the wondering was over and on this occasion I wasn't going past the stadium.

The excitement was building up and the sight of the Wimbledon fans draped in yellow and blue making their way towards the ground sent a tingle down the spine. The hardy contingent of 7,000 fans which turned up at Plough Lane every other week had suddenly swelled to 20,000. Mind you, when we began the drive down Wembley Way it was a case of 'spot the Wimbledon fan' because on both sides of the road it seemed to be a mass of red and white. The lads on the coach got quite excited when we spotted a yellow and blue scarf amidst the sea of red!

As the coach pulled into the tunnel a lump came to my throat as, out of the window, I could see my brother Peter with my eldest son Nicky on his shoulders. And there alongside them was my mother, May, and father, Dick, who was there to see me play a professional match for the first time ever. He didn't really want to go to Wembley but it was important to me for him to be there with the rest of the family. By the time I'd got off the coach my brother had managed to get inside the tunnel away from the crush which had formed outside and which had almost thrown him and Nicky in front of our coach. In fact Mum was holding on to Pete's shirt so tight to prevent him falling that the material ripped. Nicky was terrified by it all and was crying his eyes out by the time I reached him. I gave him a hug to try and comfort him and it was good to see him on this day of all days because whenever I leave home for a game he always kisses me and says: 'Good luck, Daddy. I hope you win.' It's little things like that which mean a lot and as the TV cameras were rolling at the time it will always be there on film to look back on.

From then on it was one emotional moment after another, the next being the traditional pitch walk in our suits. Even with an hour to go before kick-off, the atmosphere and the noise made your hair stand on end. Well it did mine, I'm not so sure about Corky!

Once on the pitch we were quite surprised to bump into our old boss, Dave 'Harry' Bassett, who was out there in his role as TV expert. He had done so much for Wimbledon over the years and it was great to have him there, even though we were no longer 'his' team. He was delighted for everyone that we'd made it to Wembley. He had a word with most of the lads, wishing them all the best, and I recall his three words of advice to us all: 'Don't bottle it.' It was typical of Harry to show his concern and it was as though he was giving us an extra team talk. He also sent the lads a 'good luck' telegram which I read in the dressing-room along with others I received from the likes of Wally Downes, my old PE teacher, George Duck, and some friends from my schooldays.

The few minutes I spent reminiscing helped to keep the nerves at bay but by the time I was stripped and ready for action the butterflies were back – and didn't I know it. The occasion really started to take a hold of me and I spent the majority of the last 15 minutes before walking out on to the pitch in the toilet. While I was in there I could hear the fans outside singing *Abide With Me* and it was then that it really hit me what I was about to go through. The goose bumps began to show and I think I had to spend another five minutes in the loo on the strength of it. I only just made it out in time to hear Bobby Gould's final words before we stepped out into the famous tunnel to confront our illustrious opponents who were already waiting in line.

I thought I was nervous, but some of the Liverpool lads looked positively petrified. As we emerged from the dressing-room we were all still geeing each other up with words of encouragement and defiance and it seemed to take our opponents aback. They all seemed very anxious and the expression on Alan Hansen's deadpan face told the whole story. Just seeing the look of trepidation in their eyes as they prepared to take on the infamous Crazy Gang did wonders for our confidence and you could almost feel a wave of optimism sweep throughout the side. The Liverpool players waited in grim silence while on our side of the tunnel there was a constant buzz of expectancy and determination. It was then that I felt it was going to be our day and with every shout of encouragement from the likes of Vinny Jones and John Fashanu the feeling grew. From the front of the line-up I could hear the lads behind me sayings things like 'we can do this, this is going to be our day' and it clearly unsettled our opponents. Then, with the tension mounting, the psyching-up process went one stage further with Fash echoing Vinny's customary battle cry of 'Yidahoy' and I don't think Liverpool could work out what was happening. It was all part of our pre-match ritual designed to get the adrenalin pumping amongst our own players and it wasn't done to psyche Liverpool out – although if that's the effect it had then so much the better.

By the time we walked out on to the pitch and into the wall of sound we felt we already had the upper-hand over Liverpool. There was only going to be one winner after that. It was an incredible feeling as we strutted confidently, almost arrogantly, into the sunshine and even though we could only hear the chants of the Liverpool fans packed round the tunnel end we weren't overawed. As I picked out Sandra, Nicky and the family in the main stand the pride surged through me and minutes later I was on cloud nine as I was introduced to Princess Diana. As we shook hands she said: 'You're a big lad, aren't you?' Not really knowing how to answer that I said: 'I thought you would be wearing your high heels knowing what a big team we've got.' She politely pointed out the impracticality of my suggestion by explaining that her heels would have got stuck in the ground and it was then I realised what a load of rubbish I was talking. Well it's not every day you get to meet a Princess is it? With the pleasantries and the national anthem out of the way it was time for action.

This was the moment we'd all been waiting for and as the seconds ticked by to kick-off the atmosphere inside the stadium was positively electric. I had never experienced anything like it in my life. As skipper I drew first blood for Wimbledon by winning the toss and choosing to defend the tunnel end where the majority of Liverpool fans were congregated in the first half. It was a ploy I always adopted, whenever possible, when we played at Anfield where we always preferred to defend the Kop end in the opening period. The idea was that, if we were under seige in the second half, Liverpool wouldn't be attacking their mass ranks and I wouldn't have their most vociferous supporters breathing fire down my neck.

Psychologically it was another boost to us and you could tell by the way we started the game that we were less apprehensive than our more illustrious opponents who had seen it all before. We looked hungrier, more positive than Liverpool and good old Vinny set the standard with a crunching tackle on Steve McMahon in the opening minutes which pole-axed the Liverpool man. The midfield battle between the two had been built up like a Tyson fight and was seen as one of the key confrontations on the day. But, while there was clearly no love lost between them, I don't think it was a deliberate foul on Vinny's part. He was a bit late but he simply wanted to make his presence felt early on. He certainly achieved that. The ironic thing was that Vinny probably came off worse because, as his rival went down, he caught him with his elbow and opened up a cut beneath Vinny's eye. Not that it worried Jona because more importantly he had made a mental mark on McMahon who, in all honesty, didn't have a look-in after that. In that respect Vinny did a marvellous job and you could almost see the frustration creeping into McMahon's game when he tried to sort Dennis Wise out after the little fella had caught Ablett from behind. A few words were exchanged between all concerned and Fash stepped in to make a verbal contribution of his own. That was virtually the end of the aggro for the rest of the match.

Some people may have expected a war but that was never our intention. Sure, we were out there to fight for every ball and stop Liverpool playing but for the most part we achieved that within the rules of the game. It was a confrontation between two very different sides and we were determind to come out on top. More determined than Liverpool as it turned out. We had done well against them in previous meetings, never showing them any respect, and you could sense they weren't relishing this latest encounter while we were loving every minute.

Because of the way we hustled them out of their stride and put pressure on them in all areas of the field they were forced to abandon their fluent style and fight fire with fire. We didn't allow them to roll the ball out from the back and very early on Bruce Grobbelaar was forced to kick everything long, so playing into our hands. Another key factor behind our superiority was the way Dennis Wise kept John Barnes in check down their left flank. Wisey was accustomed to playing on the opposite wing and it wasn't until the Thursday before the game that Don Howe decided to switch him to the other flank to counter-act Barnesy. It was a stroke of pure genius from an England coach who knew John's game inside out. The

Dave makes a desperate save to deny Liverpool's John Barnes during the 1988 FA Cup final.

plan worked a treat and Wisey, with his insatiable appetite for work, was superb. It made me smile to think that before the final, Barnesy had been in brilliant form and everyone predicted that he would destroy us. 'The John Barnes Cup Final' as they were calling it never materialised, however, although there was one heart-stopping moment when, just as he seemed set to put Liverpool 1-0 up, he was denied by the fingertips of yours truly. Having half-blocked a deflected shot from John Aldridge seconds before it was a vital double save by me. Had Liverpool gone ahead it could have been curtains – that's why those two saves gave me more satisfaction than the penalty stop which later made history.

We had to endure another scary moment soon after when Beardsley had the ball in the net and was convinced he'd given Liverpool the lead. Unfortunately, for him at least, referee Brian Hill had blown up for a free kick in Beardsley's favour as he was fouled by Andy Thorn en route to goal. He didn't hear the whistle but I did and was happy in the knowledge that the

19

goal would be disallowed – and rightly so. Mind you, I was still disappointed he had put the ball past me because I had hoped to keep my goal perfectly intact on the day. I didn't even let a shot past me in the warm-up, that's how determined I was. The Liverpool players were naturally upset but the whistle had gone and the ref couldn't go back on his decision. The longer the game went on the more it looked as if it was going to be our day and it came as no real surprise, not to me at least, when my room-mate Lawrie Sanchez put us in front with a deft header from a pin-point free kick by Wisey.

We always felt that if Liverpool had a weakness at the back it was in the air from set plays and once again we were proved absolutely right. Sanch doesn't get many goals and when the ball went in he didn't look as though he knew how to celebrate. He just stood there waiting for someone to jump on him and Wisey duly obliged. It was an unbelievable feeling and when I pulled off another save, this time from Hansen, seconds before the half-time whistle I just knew we were going to win. But

Bruce Grobbelaar is left stranded as Lawrie Sanchez's header loops into the top corner for Wimbledon's FA Cup winner.

it was important that we didn't get carried away and that we kept our shape and our discipline in the second half. That was the essence of Bobby Gould's team talk at half-time – at least I think it was. As we sat with our heads wrapped in ice cold towels (another brilliant Don Howe idea) we couldn't hear much of what Bob was saying, although I'm sure it would have been something like, 'if you keep playing the way you are, the cup's yours'.

Don's towel trick, one he'd used with the England squad in Mexico, worked a treat because it really cooled your head after it had taken a 45-minute pounding from the hot sun. It enabled you to think clearly again, although we must have looked a peculiar sight. I remember lifting my towel at one point and looking across the dressing-room to see a row of white towels sitting on top of sweat-stained Wimbledon shirts with players puffing and panting beneath. It would have made an interesting picture.

We felt suitably refreshed and fired up once more as we marched back up the Wembley tunnel knowing that we were just 45 minutes away from creating history. What I didn't know at the time was that I would be making my own piece of history in the process by becoming the first 'keeper to save a penalty in an FA Cup final at Wembley. By rights though I should never have had that honour because there was no way in this world that the referee should have awarded a spot-kick against us in the first place. The decision was given against Clive Goodyear when he slid in front of John Aldridge to poke the ball back at me. I could see it was a perfectly good tackle – and the video recording supported my argument – but as soon as I heard the whistle go I feared the worst. We all ran after Brian Hill to stage our protests and some of the lads, Eric Young in particular, completely lost their heads. There was a real danger that someone would get sent off so I did my best to calm them down and usher them away from the ref. Once I'd cleared the lads away I went back to remonstrate with the official once more, insisting that it wasn't a penalty. My efforts were in vain and a penalty it was.

Dave and Wimbledon defender Eric Young remonstrate with Cup final referee Brian Hill after the Dons had conceded a second-half penalty.

Suddenly the onus, along with a million eyes and more, was on me to keep our FA Cup dream alive. I'd seen John Aldridge take penalties many times in the past – he'd scored one against Forest in the semis – and I knew that he did a little shuffle before taking his kick in order to commit the 'keeper to making the first move. I remember thinking to myself: 'Wait for the shuffle, then go.' Just as Aldridge put the ball on the spot Andy Thorn went over to tell him I was going to save the kick and at the time all I could hear was, 'You're gonna miss, you're gonna miss.' It was all psychology on Thorny's part and it must have had an effect on Aldridge. All the time this was going on I stood on my goal-line attempting to compose myself and desperately trying to put some oxygen back in my lungs. All the excitement, tension and anger of the previous few minutes had left me breathless and it took me a while to get my concentration level back to what it needed to be. I took up my position on the line and waited. Aldridge stepped up and, as I expected, he produced the infamous shuffle. But I wasn't

Dave has saved John Aldridge's penalty and team-mate John Fashanu is ever-so-slightly overjoyed.

going to be fooled the way Steve Sutton had been in the semis and I waited until the last possible second before throwing myself to the left. It was suggested that I moved before the ball was kicked and I have to confess I did, not to the side though, just a pace forward to provide a better launching pad for my dive. Aldridge struck his shot reasonably well to my left but I guessed correctly and even managed to get both hands to the ball. I joked afterwards that I should have held it but at the time I was just happy to push the ball away from danger.

In fact, to describe my emotion at the time simply as 'happy' would be the understatement of the century. I was absolutely ecstatic and as the ball ran away for a corner I kept saying to myself, 'I've saved it, I've ******* saved it.' Wisey and Fash were even more excited than me, leaping all over the place and wearing the biggest grins you've ever seen. I had to calm them down before the corner was taken – after all I'd been through I didn't want us to concede a goal now. With the adrenalin still pumping I made up my mind that I would go for the ball whatever and I was relieved to see Barnes drop a poor corner on my near post. There was hardly a Liverpool shirt in sight. I must have been too casual though because I dropped the simplest catch I had to make all day and needed to fall quickly on the loose ball to avert any danger. As the TV commentary team pointed out at the time, it was quite incredible that I could go from making such a superb save to committing such an elementary mistake in the space of a few seconds. Looking back, that was the only disappointing aspect of the whole day – but it was the last thing on my mind as time ticked by and FA Cup glory beckoned.

In truth, Liverpool hardly troubled me again after the penalty (Aldridge certainly didn't because he was substituted soon after) and it wasn't just a case of us hanging on until the final whistle either. We had a few chances ourselves late on which, if converted, would have put the result beyond doubt . . . and made the last few minutes slightly more bearable. When the final whistle was eventually blown the feeling of relief, elation and pride was different to anything I'd ever known and has to be experienced to be explained. For a few seconds it was as though I was in a world of my own, running around my penalty area with arms aloft saying to myself over and over again: 'We've won it.' After a while I became aware of all the other lads, especially Thorny who leapt all over me in unashamed joy.

The scenes were incredible with players and staff congratulating each other as the Liverpool lads sat disconsolately in the centre circle. I went over to extend my commiserations to Bruce Grobbelaar who, having done a newspaper article before the final in which he asked, 'Wimbledon, they play tennis don't they?', presented me with a case containing a pair of racket-shaped glasses. I think he'd hoped to give them to me under different circumstances but I appreciated the gesture nevertheless. We agreed to exchange jerseys back in the dressing-room and it turned out that I was the only Wimbledon player to get my hands on a Liverpool shirt.

I then shook hands with each of Bruce's team-mates before setting off on the most emotional journey of my life – up the

Anyone for tennis? Dave shows off the glasses presented to him by Liverpool's Bruce Grobbelaar after the 1988 final.

famous Wembley steps to collect the FA Cup. They weren't the same steps ascended by most of my predecessors but the important thing was that we'd won the cup and I was the one to receive the trophy. As I took it from Princess Diana I raised it proudly over my head and as I did so let out a resounding cry of 'Aye, Aye' – a popular Wimbledon saying of the time. Right behind me was little Wisey who was considerably more vociferous as he let out an ear-piercing yell of 'Aye, aye, you b******s'. Right in front of the Princess too! Nice one, Wisey!

From then on it was one long celebration party which began with the customary lap of honour that left me with a lump in my throat and tears welling up in my eyes. It was particularly moving to see Harry hanging out of the commentary box high up in the gantry roaring his approval and offering his own congratulations. As we walked beneath him we held the trophy up as if to say, 'There you go mate, that's for you too.' This was Bobby Gould's team but our moment of triumph, the greatest in the club's history, was as much down to Harry as anyone and

The look of sheer delight on Dave's face tells the whole story. Dennis Wise and Andy Thorn join in the celebrations.

we wanted to let him know that we hadn't forgotten what he'd done for Wimbledon FC.

After completing a seemingly endless round of Press interviews I finally made my way back to the dressing-room about 30 minutes later to find scenes of pandemonium. There were people everywhere and it was funny to see some of the lads wandering about in the all-together in front of the Mayoress of Wimbledon. She didn't seem to mind though. To put the icing on the cake for me I was also presented with the match ball by Bobby Gould who explained that it was customary for it to go to the winning captain. Sanch looked a bit sick and asked: 'Doesn't it go to the scorer of the winning goal?' It was another magnificent memento to go with the winners' medal and the memories of a quite extraordinary day, the events of which eclipsed my wildest of dreams. Even as a starry-eyed kid with the most fertile of imaginations I'd never conjured up anything quite like this.

CHAPTER TWO

A Star in the Making

When I made my entry into the world on 20 March 1959 I wouldn't think that Mum considered for a second that she had just given birth to a boy who would go on to make history. From the moment I was born in the Park Royal Hospital, and right throughout my childhood, I was a normal lad leading a normal life. Like most football-loving kids, I had a dream of becoming a professional player and one day winning the FA Cup. Fortunately for me that dream came true. But in those football-crazy schooldays in the North London borough of Brent I was more preoccupied with scoring goals than stopping them. Yes, Britain's most expensive goalkeeper (the man who saved a penalty in an FA Cup final at Wembley), was a hungry striker whose ambition was to score goals for QPR or England! Well, we can all dream, can't we?

Most of my earliest recollections of my childhood are dominated by football, whether it was kicking a ball about in the street, playing for the school team or watching my Rangers' idols down at Loftus Road. I was quite simply soccer-mad – as the whole family (Mum and Dad, brother Pete and sisters Sue and Linda) would testify. Right through junior school at Oldfield Road, and up until the sixth form at Willesden

High, I was a prolific centre-forward who just couldn't seem to stop scoring goals. In one game, which the school team won 12-0, I scored ten – and achievements like that weren't a rarity either.

When I wasn't playing football I could normally be found at Loftus Road marvelling at the skills of my first real soccer hero – Rodney Marsh. One of the first games I went to see was against Birmingham on a day when Rodney scored a spectacular hat-trick in a superb 5-1 win. I was hooked on him and Rangers from then on. Later on Stan Bowles took on the mantle of the great entertainer and like Rodney he was a joy to watch. Just to witness the skills of those two players was worth the entrance fee alone – not that I ever paid to get in! I normally sought free admission by using my brother-in-law's lottery agent's pass and on one occasion, when we played West Ham in the FA Cup, I got in for nothing by climbing over a gate and watching the match from the top of a wall. I was prepared to do anything to see my heroes play and fortunately I never got caught.

Like a lot of kids I would wait around after the game to collect autographs and gaze admiringly up at my heroes but it wasn't until I took part in a 'Penalty Prize' competition at a local fete that I got to meet a player and say anything more than, 'Can I have your autograph please?' That was Britain's most expensive 'keeper at the time, Phil Parkes, and I would never have believed that some 14 years on I would be a record transfer 'keeper too. Together with my goalkeeping brother Pete, Phil was called on to keep goal during the penalty competition and, fancying myself as a bit of a goalscorer, I was looking forward to putting a few past him. I wasn't allowed to shoot against my brother for obvious reasons so on each occasion I came up against Phil – with some success too. I put four penalties out of five past him in the first round and eventually went on to win the competition . . . with the assistance of the big man. The kid I was playing against in the final was a cocky so-and-so and because of his arrogance Phil took an instant dislike to him and, before the final, vowed: 'I'll show him.' He hadn't really thrown himself about until that point but promptly produced a string of saves to teach the lad a lesson.

It was great to win the competition but the highlight of the day was getting the chance to talk to Phil in the dressing-room afterwards. He even took the time to offer me a few words of wisdom on how to break into professional football. From them on he was my hero. One piece of advice I remember him offering me was to avoid being as cocky as my young opponent had just been. His audacity had cost him dear and it was something I could learn from. Nowadays, whenever I'm asked by magazines and newspapers to name my childhood hero, Phil Parkes and not Rodney Marsh is the one I list. Funny thing is that, whenever I see him now, he jokes: 'You'll have to stop naming me as your childhood hero, you're making me sound even older than I am.'

Although Phil became my new hero, it wasn't just my admiration for him which led to my transformation from a scorer to a stopper. As I got older my goal-scoring prowess counted for little because by then I was considered too small (about five feet eight inches) and skinny for a centre-forward and was moved back into midfield. Even with the best will in the world I wasn't a midfield player, but it wasn't until I was pushing 17 that I found my niche in the game I loved . . . as a goalkeeper. Before then I'd only ever played between the sticks in the street or down the park, throwing myself around in the mud, but it was never any more than that. Not until the school goalkeeper left and we couldn't find a replacement, that is. Nobody else was willing to take on the job so I decided to give it a go. I did quite well in that first game and, with a little persuasion, agreed to carry on in goal. Mind you, as captain, I remember ordering one of the outfield players to swap positions with me midway through one game we were losing 3-0. I thought to myself, 'I'll show 'em how to score goals', and promptly marched up front to demonstrate the art of putting the ball in the back of the net. We lost 9-0. From then on I decided to stick to goalkeeping and it has proved to be one of the best decisions I've ever made.

I considered myself a good outfield player but I doubt

whether I would have made the grade as a striker. One lad from Willesden High who did, however, was Luther Blissett. He was two years older than me (and probably still is!) and had that happy knack of scoring goals which was to make him such a great favourite at Watford. Luther, together with the likes of Gary Locke, Brian Stein, Steve Gatting (cricketer Mike's brother) and Ricky Hill all lived within a stone's throw of our house in Brent and it's incredible to think that one small area of London should produce so many would-be professional footballers.

Because we played all our school matches on a Saturday, however, we were never available to play for the County whose teams also turned out at weekends. I never played any representative football at all during my schooldays which made it doubly difficult for me to break into non-League or professional soccer. Scouts could always be seen on the touch-line at County matches but rarely came to school games, so my chances of getting spotted were virtually non-existent. I was still determined to become a pro-footballer though, despite constant discouragement from teachers and careers officers alike. At one stage I asked my PE teacher, Dave Evans, to write to QPR for me to request a trial (either as an outfield player or a 'keeper) but he warned me not to build my hopes up too high and, sure enough, nothing came of it.

The set-back didn't deter me and football continued to take priority over my schoolwork. I wasn't a bad pupil but it used to annoy Mum and Dad that the only subject in which I obtained top marks was Physical Education. I always receiving glowing reports from the PE master but with the other subjects it was usually a case of 'could do better'. Languages were never my forte, in fact I was so bad at German and French that I was delighted to obtain CSE grades of four and five when I sat my exams. I thought the best I could have hoped for was unclassified.

I could, and probably should, have studied harder but for all my academic shortcomings I was never what you would term a rebel or a tearaway. I didn't get into too much trouble (no more than the average boy at any rate) and rarely became involved in fights – apart from with my brother, that is. We were always pulling on the boxing gloves and scrapping in the house. It was usually quite competitive too, especially on the day when he knocked me out cold with a jab Mike Tyson would be proud of. I walked straight into the punch, having bounced off a mattress which was upright against the wall. It must have looked like something out of a cartoon programme as I slithered slowly down the wall with blood trickling from my nose.

As a kid though I was, by and large, quite shy – off the football field at least – and when I bumped into an old schoolmate years later having made it to the top in football, he remarked on the striking transformation in my personality. We met at a presentation dinner and he was amazed that a lad who, at one time, wouldn't have said boo to a goose was now a national celebrity oozing confidence. It's all down to the experience I've picked up during my footballing career which kicked off in very modest fashion when I left school at 17.

My first club was a school-leavers' side with the unforgettable name of 'The Old Uffintonians' and turning out for their seventh XI provided me with the humblest of starts to my career. It also signalled my arrival on the drinking scene! After games we could normally be found propping up the nearest bar and I soon came to realise that a relaxing drink following a match was as much a part of the day as the football itself.

When I left school at 17 I was a five-foot-eight-inch stick insect carrying marginally more fat than a greasy chip, but within a year of stepping nervously out into the big wide world I had grown an incredible six inches. Not a bad thing for a budding goalkeeper to do, you might think, but the trouble was that I ended up looking even more like a bean pole than ever before. When I bumped into old schoolmates who hadn't seen me for the previous 12 months they couldn't believe the change in me. In fact, some didn't even recognise me at all and would say things like, 'I'm sure I know you from somewhere', or, 'You look like Dave Beasant'. It took me some time to convince them I was Dave Beasant, the same scrawny youth they'd shared a classroom with all those years. I became a little conscious of my size, height and weight (or lack of it), and it wasn't until I joined Wimbledon that I began filling out as a result of a weight training programme Harry Bassett set for me. I became a lot broader across the shoulders but, unfortunately, my legs didn't show the same willingness to co-operate. My hairstyle also changed quite dramatically. At school it was always greased back (I was a real Brylcreem boy) and gave the impression of being straight. When I met my wife, Sandra, she encouraged me to 'let it go' and my natural curls were unleashed on the world – again much to the surprise of people I hadn't seen for a while. They were convinced I'd had a Kevin Keegan-style perm, but it was natural – honest.

From the Uffintonians I joined a Sunday team, Legion-naires, who were short of a 'keeper and asked me to help them out on a temporary basis. They were one of the top Sunday sides in the area and I shared some success with them, not to mention a few hangovers on the morning of the match after a heavy Saturday night. Although I didn't realise it at the time this was the first of my links with Dave Bassett who, a few years before, had played for Legionnaires' great rivals Langford. I never played against him of course and never saw him play but I used to hear all about him and the grudge matches between the two teams. Everyone knew Harry because of what he went on to achieve and it wasn't too long before I was hearing all the Legionnaires v Langford stories first hand.

After 18 months of Sunday morning football I took my first positive steps towards realising my dream when Edgware Town from the Athenian League came in for me. The club's assistant manager had seen me playing for Legionnaires against a Sunday team he ran and was impressed enough to invite me down to play for Edgware Reserves. I played for the second string for a time and did well enough to convince them I was worthy of a first-team debut when the regular goalkeeper was unavailable for a London Senior Cup tie because of work commitments.

Ironically, my first game was against, of all clubs, Wimble-don. It was around the time that The Dons were building a reputation as FA Cup giant-killers and, even though they were a non-League team too at that stage, it was seen as a big game for Edgware. Although we lost 2-0 on the day, I received quite a bit of praise for the part I played in keeping the score down to a respectable level. But, if I was being honest, I'd have to put a lot of my success down more to the huge square goal-posts which saved me on a number of occasions than to my own brilliance. It was the first time I had played in front of a 'big' crowd (about 500 or so) and it was also the first occasion that I'd been subjected to hostility from opposing supporters. For a start the Wimbledon fans took the mickey out of a corduroy hat I'd borrowed from a local reporter to keep the sun out of my eyes (mind you, on seeing photographs of myself later, I did look a bit of a wally, like someone they'd dragged off the street to keep goal for them). I didn't really mind the mickey-taking but the thing that took me aback was when a fan, for want of a better word, threw a battery (an HP11 or something similar) at me. Had it struck me in the eye it could have caused a nasty injury.

On the whole, though, I emerged from my first 'real' match with my pride intact – and with the promise of my first wage packet for playing football. After my second game a week later I was handed a brown envelope and inside was the princely sum of £3. It may not have seemed much but at the time it meant everything to me. I was being paid for doing something I loved. By the start of the following season, when I was 18 and a first-team regular, I was earning £8 per match plus £2 win bonus. On top of the £50 a week I was earning as a screen printer it made me quite a wealthy young man.

I must have done well in my first season at Edgware because I was named 'Player of the Year' at the end of it, an award which I took home and proudly showed to brother Pete, himself a 'keeper. Being four years older than me had had already amassed quite a collection of trophies and medals from playing in the local Leagues but, to me, my award topped the lot. When I showed him my trophy I said something like 'Now that's what you call an award'. It was a light-hearted ritual we were to go through time and again later in my career as I added to my collection during the glory days with Wimbledon.

Pete was half an inch taller than me and about two feet wider (it would have taken about ten minutes to run round him!) and, on his day, not a bad 'keeper. He could have perhaps progressed further in the game but for a series of bad injuries which held him back. I remember watching an important cup game in which he dislocated his shoulder in a collision with an opposing forward and being called on by his desperate boss to replace him. I was a Wimbledon player at the time, not a first-team regular though, and just recovering from a broken finger so I was a bit wary about playing in a game that didn't really concern me. But I was so annoyed about the reckless challenge which had put my brother out of action that I agreed to stand in for him. When I went on to the field I made it my first task to go up to the fella who'd floored Pete and tell him in no uncertain terms: 'Come at me like that and I know who'll come off second best – and it won't be me'. Fighting talk indeed. It wasn't like me to react in that way but the sight of my brother being carried off to hospital as white as a sheet and shaking with pain brought out the aggression in me. And it worked too, because the player never came near the area let alone me for the rest of the match. We won 1-0 and I was pleased to help Pete's team through to the next round of the Cup but, in hindsight, it wasn't a very sensible thing to do. I could have damaged my finger again and, had Wimbledon found out, I would have been in big trouble.

It was an act of impulse similar to the one which once threatened to ruin all the good work I'd done at Edgware prior to joining Wimbledon. After winning the 'Player of the Year' award in my first season I was invited to have trials with Walthamstow, a bigger club playing in a better standard of football in the Isthmian League. It meant I had to travel a lot further to train and play each week but, because it was another step up the ladder, I decided to go along and play in a few pre-season games for them, one of which was a 1-1 draw with West Ham's reserves. After about half-a-dozen appearances for Walthamstow I began to tire of all the travelling to and from the ground (often through rush hour traffic) all the way around the notorious North Circular road. I decided to return to Edgware only to find my place had been filled by a promising new 'keeper. Faced with this dilemma I was almost tempted to try my luck with another well-known Isthmian League club, Hayes, whose manager Martin Hackett invited me along to a midweek match for talks. After the game we were having a chat when a giant, black player built like the proverbial brick s*** house walked past us. Martin pointed to him and said: 'That's Cyrille Regis, I'm selling him to West Brom next week.' He assured me that Football League scouts were regular visitors to Hayes and did his best to convince me that my chances of being spotted would be greater with them than Edgware.

What he said made a lot of sense but for some reason I just didn't fancy the move and I decided to stay and fight for my place at Edgware who had just sold Brian Stein, his brother Edwin and a lad called Michael Sperring to Luton. The talk at the time was that Luton would be back at the end of the season to get me but, in the meantime, my first priority was to get back into the Edgware team. Fortunately, for me at least, the 'keeper who had been bought to replace me picked up an injury soon afterwards and I was back in the team. It was a very lucky break for me, especially as, within another few weeks, I was attracting the attention of Dave Bassett, then assistant manager to Dario Gradi at Wimbledon. I had been recommended to him by Brian Hall, Wealdstone manager and Wimbledon scout, and he came along to see what all the fuss was about. I later learned that it wasn't me they had originally intended to sign but a black player called Peter Shadindi. In the games they came to watch him, however, I must have impressed them because I was the one Wimbledon ended up signing while Peter drifted into obscurity.

That break represented quite a dramatic turnaround for me because only a few weeks before, as I couldn't get a game for Edgware, I was turning out for Guinness' third team playing against the likes of my brother's company side Heinz. Between us we used to eat and drink well but it was a lethal combination, if you see what I mean! To go from that standard of football to a Fourth Division Club in less than a month was nothing short

of incredible and as soon as I knew Wimbledon were in for me
my mind was made up.

Things began to happen after Edgware had played Billericay
when one of our players, Geoff Booth, told me that Dave
Bassett was outside and wanted to talk to me. I still had
my kit on but didn't bother to change and rushed outside to
find this fella wearing the sort of sheepskin coat I had always
imagined managers of League clubs to wear (in fact I think
Harry's still got it). When I approached him he was looking
almost as sheepish as his coat and mumbled something like: 'I
can't speak to you yet, son. I've got to talk to your manager.' I
didn't really understand why at the time but I suspect he didn't
want to be accused of making an illegal approach. It was all
new and somewhat sinister to me then and reluctantly I went
back to the dressing-room a little confused but as excited as a
kid at Christmas. The upshot of it all was that I was invited to
train with Wimbledon for a few days a week and play for the
reserves. I needed to take time off work at the printers and I
can remember my first day as though it was yesterday.

Edgware manager Dave Finn had arranged to meet me
outside the bingo hall near my home at eight thirty a.m. to
drive me to Wimbledon's training ground, and I made sure
I was there with plenty of time to spare. I didn't want to
leave anything to chance. By nine o'clock Dave still hadn't
arrived and all sorts of crazy things were going through my
mind: I've missed him; he's forgotten about me; I'm going
to miss the training session; I've blown my big chance. I ran
home to telephone him at his house but there was no reply so
I rushed back to the bingo hall and there was still no sign of
him.

At about nine-fifteen he rolled up as calm as you like with
the explanation that we didn't have to be there until ten.
He reckoned we still had plenty of time on our hands, but
that was eaten by the extra miles we had to travel trying to
find the training ground. By then I was a nervous wreck
wondering whether I would ever get my trial. I needn't have
worried because I wasn't required to train with the lads in
the morning as I was down to play in a reserve match in the

afternoon. All that rushing round and panicking had been for nothing.

The game itself, against Peterborough reserves, went very well and although I didn't have too much to do I managed to keep a clean sheet in a goalless draw. I made a few good saves but what impressed Wimbledon most, I think, were my big, booming goalkicks which have since played a telling part in my rise to the top. For the next month I was asked to train with Wimbledon, playing for their reserves in midweek but still turning out for Edgware on a Saturday. At the end of the trial period Harry said he was keen to sign me on a year's contract but explained that Dario Gradi, his boss and the man with the final say on the matter, still had reservations about me. It wasn't until Dario asked goalkeeping coach Mike Kelly, a former QPR player, to have one last look at me in a reserve game at Brighton that the door to League football finally opened wide. It was on the basis of his verdict ('for a big fella he moves his feet well, he's got a good pair of hands and he's worth giving a chance') that Dario agreed to sign me on.

I didn't know at the time that Mike was running the rule over me but after the game (which we won 3-2) Harry, who had taken us all for a drink in the Hove pub near the ground, pulled me to one side and said that I was to be offered a year's contract. He asked me how much I was earning at the printers and he said that the club would match my £50-a-week wages. To me that was a brilliant offer. It wasn't until later, much later, that I realised that I had actually agreed to take quite a cut in salary because I would no longer be receiving the extra £10 a week I got playing for Edgware. At the time, though, I think I would have agreed to play for nothing. I went home as high as a kite to break the news to everyone, still buzzing with the excitement of becoming a professional footballer. Dave Beasant was on his way.

CHAPTER THREE

From Superflop to Super Don

I signed for Wimbledon in March 1979 – the year the club was promoted to the Third Division for the first time – and I had to wait just nine months for my big chance in the senior side. When it came – on 12 January 1980 – I was determined to make the most of it: but to say my first steps up the soccer ladder were tentative would be an understatement to end all understatements. My debut against Blackpool was a nightmare, an unmitigated disaster which I feared had wrecked my football career almost before it had begun. Instead of making my ascent up the so-called ladder to stardom I put my big size nines through the first rung and promptly came crashing back down to earth. This is going to be painful, but let me explain.

My opportunity came about because first choice 'keeper Ray Goddard had to cry off because of a back injury – the trouble was that I didn't know I was playing until the morning of the game. While that meant I didn't have to spend days worrying about making my debut, it also meant that I'd had little or no time to prepare myself properly for what was the most important game of my life. To make matters worse I'd spent the previous night at the cinema and capped the evening with a few beers down the pub. Although I didn't get drunk I'd had more to drink that you would normally have the night before a big game. When Ray phoned me at home in the morning to say he was struggling and that I would be in the team my first thoughts were, 'Oh no, I shouldn't have had those beers last night.' When the game was over and I was sitting in the dressing-room brooding about Blackpool's winning goal which I'd let through my legs I vowed never to drink again before a match.

I put my mistake, an elementary 'keeper's error, down to my poor preparation and following our 2-1 defeat – in front of our own fans too – I was virtually inconsolable. All sorts of desperate thoughts were racing through my mind, not least the fear that I'd blown my big chance. I apologised to Dario, the boss, and the rest of the players but they were all great about it, refusing to blame me for the defeat – to my face at least. The ironic thing was that before the game the chairman at the time, Ron Noades, had assured me that everyone had every confidence in me, but added: 'Knowing you, you'll have a nightmare on your debut.' Prophetic words indeed. Afterwards I remarked on his gloomy forecast as we shared a drink in the directors' lounge where the lads, in an attempt to drown my misery, kept plying me with champagne. It was as though I'd played a blinder in the Cup final or something and I went home slightly the worse for wear. It was good to know everyone had forgiven me for committing the cardinal sin, although I later discovered that on the strength (or weakness) of my performance Dario had instructed Harry to go out and find the club a new 'keeper. The boss, apparently, wasn't convinced that I had the right temperament and after just 90 minutes of League football my future was in doubt.

Thankfully Wimbledon showed a bit of faith in me by not buying another 'keeper and a few weeks later I was back in the team to play Plymouth because Ray was suspended, having been sent off after a game against Mansfield for protesting about a goal he'd conceded. This time, I decided, my preparations were going to be perfect and from the Tuesday to the Saturday not an ounce of alcohol passed my lips. I went from one extreme to another and my cautiousness paid off because I had a good game and we won 3-1. I was delighted because, having made such a hash of my debut, there was even more pressure on me to do well. I had to prove, to myself as much as anyone, that I was good enough and as the only goal I conceded was a penalty my confidence was restored. My debut day disaster was behind me and I was able to look to the future with considerably more optimism than before.

My performance wasn't enough to keep my place in the side, however, because the following week Ray was back in the team and I remained in the reserves for the rest of the season. Sadly the club was relegated back to the Fourth Division at the end of it, having been bottom of the table since November. To add to the disappointment I broke a bone in my hand in an end-of-season friendly against Crystal Palace so my first experiences of professional football were anything but memorable.

The following season the boss, not surprisingly, kept faith with Ray but after just five games during which he had conceded seven goals I made my return . . . on merit this time. My first game of the 1980-81 season was at Crewe in September (we won 3-0) and it proved to be the start of a 31-match run which ended at Darlington in March. On the afternoon of the midweek game we were booked into an hotel for a pre-match rest, only there weren't many of us who managed four winks let alone 40. There were a few inter-room fights going on with water being thrown everywhere and, although we thought it was fun, Harry, who took over from Dario in the summer, was far from happy. He warned us to 'beat Darlington or else'. We were hammered 4-1! The game provided me with my first experience of a fiery Scot called David Speedie – and painful it was too. Early on he gave me one hell of a whack on my knee which left me hobbling around my penalty area in agony for some time afterwards. Because of the injury to my right leg I was forced to take all kicks with my left, with the result that they were barely clearing my area let alone the half-way line. After one particularly miserable effort our sub Paul Denny ran around to my goal with a message from the bench which went something like: 'Harry says buck your ideas up or you're off.'

I couldn't believe it, he was seriously considering substituting the goalkeeper.

Three days later I was out of the team altogether, although not because of my performance at Darlington. I broke my finger in a training accident (on my birthday too) and was forced to miss the next six matches. I came back to help us clinch promotion to Division Three towards the end of the season before standing down for the final match which had been earmarked as Ray's last for the club. In typical Wimbledon fashion he went out in style by scoring from the penalty spot.

So with Ray hanging his gloves up the chance was there the following season for me to make the first-team jersey my own and, as if to confirm my position as the club's number one keeper, I was voted 'Player of the Year' by the fans. With Third Division football to look forward to the following season my summer break was a happy one and I spent most of it savouring my early success. My disastrous debut was well and truly a thing of the past and I was a fully fledged member of the team – and the 'Super Dons', as a group of the club's characters became known. The thing that I'd noticed above all else about Wimbledon in the short time I'd been at Plough Lane was the way the people at the club, players and management alike, brought out the character in those around them. If I was a little shy and wary on joining Wimbledon it didn't last long and the lads soon enticed me out of my shell and taught me how to express myself. Once you responded you were part of the team, one of the lads, or a member of the 'family' as it became known.

I didn't have too much trouble settling in and knew I'd been accepted when the jokers – people like Steve Parsons and Wally Downes – made me the butt of their pranks. When I first joined the club I travelled to work on a motorbike (a Yamaha 125) complete with full-faced helmet and elbow length gauntlets. Needless to say my machine and my attire became the source of much merriment among the lads and on more than one occasion I came in from training to find my crash helmet full of talcum powder. Because it was foam lined it was impossible to get all the talc out each time and, more often than not, I would arrive home with grey hair. I didn't really mind because pranks like that made for a happy atmosphere in the dressing-room. Even playing for the reserves in the very early days was fun because we had so many characters, players who stayed with the club and later formed the basis of the first team which brought such remarkable success to Plough Lane.

The motorbike jokes didn't last for long though because Dario made me sell my pride and joy and buy a car to be more in keeping with my role as a professional footballer. He also explained that, as my hands were the tools of my trade, I was putting them at risk every time I took off on my bike. I wasn't happy about it, particularly as I was going to be spending a lot more money on petrol, but I could understand his thinking. I'd already had one potentially nasty accident when I was lucky to escape with a few grazes and bruises after ramming a car and flying over the handle bars. At the time I thought nothing of it (I was more concerned about a clock radio I had just bought and was carrying under my jacket) but realised later that one crash could end my playing career. Giving up my bike was a small price to pay for being a professional footballer, the life of which was every bit as good as I'd imagined – even at a small club like Wimbledon. Okay, so the facilities weren't that clever and Plough Lane was little better than a non-League ground, but just being a full-time footballer meant the world to me.

Financially, times were hard for the club and I remember how Dave Bassett always referred to us as 'Scraggy-arse Rovers' but I was doing what I'd always wanted to do and I intended to savour everything that happened, no matter how small or seemingly insignificant. In those early days one of my biggest thrills was receiving my first club jumper with Wimbledon FC sewn into it. From being a nobody I suddenly felt I was a somebody, a footballer with the chance to make a name for myself. Maybe I was too enthusiastic about it all and perhaps my feelings were a bit over-the-top.

It's certainly fair to say I allowed my new-found status to go to my head somewhat. I would walk into a pub or a club wearing my Wimbledon jumper thinking I was some kind of local celebrity people knew or wanted to know. If I was out with my old mates from school and there were a few girls around I would be thinking things like, 'Well, if they fancy any of us it's going to be me because I'm a pro-footballer.' I got too wrapped up in the image and, although I didn't show off with the other players, looking back, I was a bit too cocky when I was out without them. It wasn't until my girlfriend, Sandra, ditched me two weeks after we started going out together because I was 'too big-headed' that I began to realise the error of my ways. I used to think I was someone to be looked up to and it took me a while to realise my attitude was all wrong. I hadn't achieved anything by then and my inexperience on the field was, if anything, surpassed only by my naivety off it. Thankfully I later managed to convince Sandra I wasn't the arrogant so-and-so she first thought and we've been together ever since.

I was soon made aware of the need to socialise with people without impressing on them the fact that I was a pro-footballer. And, at a club where there was plenty of socialising to be done, that was important. The funny thing was that when I left Edgware to go professional with Wimbledon I thought I was turning my back on all the fun, the laughing and joking that went with playing for a non-League club. But I'd been at Plough Lane virtually five minutes when I realised I was going to have even more fun at Wimbledon. The atmosphere, the banter, the camaraderie was all better than I'd ever experienced.

Mind you, my willingness to have a bit of fun during training backfired on me on one occasion when Dario was in charge. It was early on in the 1980-81 season when we played Sheffield Wednesday in the League Cup and we'd taken a 2-1 lead to Hillsborough for the second leg. We lost 3-1 on the night and were sent crashing out of the competition, having had another famous giant-killing act within our grasp. Two of their goals were down to the 'keeper and afterwards Dario wasn't a happy man. He burst into the dressing-room, hurling torrents of abuse as he did so, and pointed an accusing finger at me saying: 'It's all your fault.' The thing I found incredible was that I hadn't even been playing and was sitting there in my suit and tie thinking he was picking on the wrong fella. He went into a lengthy explanation to the effect that if I'd have worked harder in training (instead of getting sucked into the 'Wally Downes syndrome') I would have been in the team that night and possibly wouldn't have conceded the goals Ray had done.

I couldn't believe that I was getting the blame for a defeat in a match I hadn't even played in and I still get reminded of the incident today. Dario's rollicking did teach me a lesson though and prompted me to buck my ideas up in training from then on. The extra work I put in paid dividends and, having tucked 34 League games under my belt that season (1980-81) I was ready to impose my authority on the Third Division. Although I obviously didn't realise it at the time, our first game of the 1981-82 season in Division Three was to be the start of a run in the Wimbledon first team which only ended when I left the club after the 1988 FA Cup final. I never missed a match in between times, a consecutive run of over 300 League games. The first of those was, however, a nightmare (a 4-1 defeat at Swindon) and the second wasn't much better – a 3-1 reverse at home to Millwall. There were a lot of question marks against us even then. In fact we went nine games that season without a win and it soon became clear that the team we had was too good for the Fourth Division but wasn't equipped for the Third. We didn't get out of the bottom four all season and it was no real surprise when we were relegated in 21st position.

The season was a nightmare, especially for Alan Cork who broke his leg after just six games, an injury that was to keep him out of the game for 18 months. To add insult to injury we were knocked out of the FA Cup at the second round hurdle by non-League Enfield. As renowned giant-killers ourselves it was a bitter pill to swallow, in fact it lodged in Harry's throat for some time afterwards. He would probably put that down as his most embarrassing defeat – and mine too – because from being 1-0 up we lost 4-1. That inept performance gave birth to his phrase of 'Charlie big potatoes' which he labelled us afterwards. By going into the game thinking that we were going to walk all over our non-League opponents we allowed

Enfield to do to Wimbledon what the club had done to League sides themselves as amateurs not so long before.

But if anything the defeat taught us a lesson we were never to forget and the following season (1982-83) saw us adopt a more professional, determined attitude which was to become the trademark of Wimbledon FC. It was the start of our great surge up through the divisions and there was never a stage during that season when we looked as though we wouldn't win promotion. In the end we won the Fourth Division Championship in style with 98 points and 96 League goals to our credit. We put together a tremendous run in the second half of the season when we lost just one game from Christmas onwards, winning 18 out of 27 matches in the process.

By the time we played our penultimate game of the season, away at Halifax, we had already won the title but it didn't deter Harry from giving us a right roasting at half-time. We came in 1-0 down and Harry went loopy, absolutely mad, saying: 'You may think you've arrived, you may think you're there, but you're wrong.' It was another of Harry's infamous sayings and whenever he said it we would always wind him up by asking: 'But where's "there" Harry?' This time he wasn't joking and we all sat with heads bowed as he stomped up and down the dressing-room with his red head on, hurling abuse at all and sundry. It wasn't easy to keep a straight face because all the time he was on the march we could see a sweet paper stuck to the sole of his shoe. He tried to kick the paper off but, in his rage, only succeeded in losing his shoe which smashed against the ceiling and landed on Stewart Evans' lap. As Stewart calmly handed the shoe back we were all bursting to laugh, but didn't dare in case Harry really did explode. As it turned out we played a lot better in the second half and, after earning a point, Harry saw the funny side of his tantrum insisting he'd been a 'mug' to carry on like that. Who were we to disagree?

The outburst was typical of him and reminded me of a funny story the lads told of Harry when, a few years before, he took the reserves on an away match to Torquay in the club's mini-bus which he drove. I wasn't on the trip but, apparently, at one stage the lads were in typically high spirits, fighting and generally clowning around in the back of the van, when suddenly someone's foot went straight through the vinyl lining of the roof. In disgust, Harry brought the van to a screeching halt and proceeded to tear into the lads saying things like: 'That's typical of you lot, you're a bunch of amateurs who will never be any better than Fourth Division standard.' Twenty minutes later, however, Harry was the one in disgrace when the van chugged to a halt on the M4. Harry had forgotten to fill it up with petrol! As the lads waited for the youngest apprentice to run two miles down the road to get some petrol a fella called Roy Davies decided to pass the time away by dancing on the roof of the van. His antics didn't go down too well with passing motorists, one of whom wrote a letter of complaint to the local paper describing the 'outrageous scenes which were typical of football'.

Harry wasn't happy with that either. Although he had a seemingly happy-go-lucky approach to management he had certain standards and he expected his players to maintain them – on and off the field. His attitude towards the game was such that we should play every match as though our lives depended on it and he would let us know in no uncertain manner if we fell short of the mark – as he had done on that day at Halifax. I had my own excuses on that occasion, having spent most of the first half in agony with a bad stomach. I called to the bench for some kaoline and morphine to quell the pain and, as I went to drink it, the Wimbledon fans behind my goal asked me if it was champagne. I turned to face them and raised the cup in mock championship celebration before downing the stuff in one to a rousing cheer. It wasn't until after the game that I discovered that my banter with the crowd hadn't gone down too well with an on-looking First Division manager who was there to run the rule over me. Harry informed me that Sheffield Wednesday boss Howard Wilkinson had been watching me but had gone away unimpressed thinking I was nothing more than a 'big-time Charlie'. Whether Harry was just winding me up or whether Mr Wilkinson had been put off by my antics with the kaoline and morphine I don't know. And I never did find out either because Wednesday were never mentioned again.

In truth it didn't worry me too much because we'd won promotion and were on our way back to the Third Division. At the time I was more concerned with our last game of the season away at Bury which was to be shown on TV. For virtually all the lads it was our first appearance in front of the television cameras so beforehand we arranged to mark our debut with something the armchair fans wouldn't forget. As we were going on holiday to Magaluf at the end of the season we agreed that, when we scored a goal, everyone would have to perform what we labelled the 'Magaluf shuffle' – a ridiculous dance to celebrate scoring. Stewart Evans struck the first goal and all the lads rushed to congratulate him when suddenly, Glyn Hodges, within earshot of the TV microphones, screamed 'shuffle' and everyone went into the dance we'd been practicing in training. People watching the game must have thought we had gone mad, but we were delighted to have scored another first for Wimbledon. We laid claim to a unique form of celebrating which other clubs eventually copied. Being at the opposite end of the field I couldn't really join in the celebrations but my moment of triumph came later when I saved a penalty and did a solo-shuffle for the cameras. A bit over the top perhaps but that was Wimbledon for you.

No-one could argue that we didn't go up in style but the question we were all asking at the time was, 'How long will we last in the Third Division this time?' The club's two previous ventures in the Third – in 1980 and 1982 – had ended in disaster with us bouncing straight back down again. I had my doubts about us lasting much longer than a season again but the general feeling within the club this time was that we were on our way. And so it seemed was I, because during that summer Stoke City (who were then in the First Division) came in for me and for a time it looked like my Wimbledon career was at an end. It wasn't the first time I'd attracted attention from a bigger club because, during the 1980-81 season, Chelsea made a £50,000 offer for me. Geoff Hurst was in charge at Stamford Bridge at the time but it was his assistant Bobby Gould who saw me as the man to solve Chelsea's defensive problems. Their bid, however, was rejected out of hand by boss Dario

Gradi and I never heard any more from them. Stoke's bold approach in the summer of 1983 was treated more seriously by Harry, however, and I was told I was free to talk to them.

Having just helped the club win promotion to the Third Division I may have surprised a few people by refusing to sign a new contract after reaching the end of my current deal. But, even in the light of the success we'd just enjoyed, I believed the time was right to move on. I had, I felt, begun to establish myself as a 'keeper of some quality and I'd set my heart on playing in the First Division. I didn't think I could achieve that with Wimbledon. I always considered the club to be a Third and Fourth Division outfit and couldn't see us going any higher. Having said that, however, I had never really pushed to get away – not until now at least. Harry had always kept me informed of any clubs that were interested in me but always managed to convince me that my future lay at Plough Lane. This particular summer though I was adamant that I'd played my last game for Wimbledon and when Stoke came in for me I was more than happy to hear what they had to say and offer.

Richie Barker was the boss but it was his assistant Bill Asprey who made the first move, calling me at home to arrange a meeting with the two of them. We met at Newport Pagnell service station and I drove up there in my brother's mark IV Cortina. I was keen to make a good impression so I used his car rather than my clapped out Ford Capri. The talks went well and, as the start of the season was just a few weeks away, I was invited to train with the Stoke lads for a week. I kept Harry informed of the developments and he immediately discouraged me from going to train with them insisting that, as I wasn't the world's best trainer, it might affect my chances of completing the transfer. Whether he was actually trying to do me a favour or not I'm not sure but to me it had the hallmark of a Harry ploy to keep me at Wimbledon. Whatever his motives I decided against going up to Stoke to train but told Richie Barker I was still keen to sign for the club. Stoke offered Wimbledon £30,000 plus their reserve team 'keeper and not surprisingly it was rejected by Harry who reckoned he could get £100,000 for me at a transfer tribunal. With that development Richie agreed to let the tribunal set the fee but, just when I thought I was about to become a Stoke player, he took me aback by adding: 'On one condition.'

The condition was that, if the tribunal set a fee above what Stoke were prepared to pay, they had the option to pull out of the deal. As I was new to the world of transfers I sought the advice of the PFA and I soon began to realise the pitfalls of a conditional tribunal. To complicate matters still further Harry had begun to put pressure on me to sort my future out because, with the start of the season just around the corner, he wanted to know where he and Wimbledon stood. He threatened to buy another goalkeeper and suggested that even if I ended up staying, my first-team place would go to the new arrival. I maintained that I wanted to play First Division football but he reckoned I would be better off getting more experience under my belt before going up to the top level. The dilemma I was faced with was whether or not to run the risk of going to tribunal (which wouldn't be until two weeks into the season) only to discover that Stoke wouldn't pay the fee, so leaving my career in limbo.

By telling me he was about to buy a replacement for me Harry was calling my bluff and forcing me to make a decision either way. It was good management on his part because he was trying to do his best for the club but it didn't help me make the toughest decision of my career. Harry did bring a lad to the club, Stuart Naylor from Lincoln, for a trial and it was a strange experience training with a fella who could well have been taking my place. Another tactical move on Harry's part. As it turned out Stuart lasted just a few hours at Wimbledon, partly because of an injury which restricted him in training but more so because the other lads had refused to accept him. As they wanted me to stay most of them completely blanked Stuart and he must have been made to feel so unwelcome. It was nice of the lads to show such loyalty towards me but that was no way to treat a fellow professional and I felt very sorry for him. The following day Harry gave them a real lambasting over Stuart's snub. You could tell he was really annoyed as he layed into them saying: 'While I am manager of this club don't ever treat a player, new or otherwise, like that again.' As it turned out I later telephoned Richie Barker to tell him I couldn't agree to go to a conditional tribunal and the saga ended with me signing a new contract at Plough Lane. It was all bitterly disappointing and, for a time, difficult to accept because I had been a whisker away from the First Division and fulfilling a childhood dream. But I was comforted by the thought that at 24 I was still young enough for other chances to come along.

CHAPTER FOUR

Against All Odds

I had never come as close to leaving Wimbledon as I had during the summer, although I had been linked with other clubs in the past. Chelsea, as I mentioned earlier was one, and rumour has it that at one stage First Division giants Liverpool and Manchester United also saw me as a potential star of the future. All very flattering but as soon as I asked Harry if there was any truth in the stories he bluntly replied: 'Don't be daft, what makes you think clubs like that would possibly be interested in you?' He had this way of bringing you back down to earth did Harry. 'You're joking, aren't you? You've got to prove yourself at this level first', was another of his retorts designed to keep your feet on the ground. He rarely praised his players and I remember on one occasion after a 6-1 win against Aldershot he came into the dressing-room and instead of complimenting us on the six goals we'd scored he had a go at us about the one we'd let in. At the end of his little lecture he did say, 'Anyway, well done, lads', at which point we all fainted before asking: 'What did you say, Harry, was that praise?' Wally would always have a go at him saying, 'Go on, Harry, squeeze out a "well done" for the lads. Say it under your breath, anything.' If he did ever issue any praise there would always be a 'but' at the end of it. 'Yes, you've done well BUT you haven't made it yet, there's still a long way to go.' The lads respected him for it though. You took notice of what he said and I always remember him telling us to use Wimbledon as a stepping stone to a bigger club. I would remind him of that when a 'bigger club' was allegedly interested in me but it didn't seem to make any difference.

I tried not to take newspaper reports linking me with the likes of Liverpool too seriously although there was a time when I thought my big moment had arrived. I received a phone call at my mother's house and on the end of the line was a fella with a gruff, Geordie accent saying his name was Bob Paisley. I couldn't believe what I was hearing as he continued: 'You've probably read the stories in the papers about us being interested in you and they are absolutely correct. We would like you to play for Liverpool.' It crossed my mind at the time that I was the victim of a major wind-up but I couldn't exactly give the caller a mouthful of abuse in case it really was Bob Paisley, so I had to go along with it. I asked him if he'd spoken to Harry and he assured me he had gone through the proper channels and had been given permission to speak to

Dave shows the style which made him a target of the First Division big boys – or so he thought.

me. I thought it strange I hadn't been informed but I told him I'd love to sign for Liverpool. How could I turn down such a golden opportunity? Although I still had a nagging doubt as to the credibility of the call I began to get quite excited about the prospect of signing for the biggest club in the country. But after three or four minutes any illusions I might have had about striking it rich were shattered when I heard this inane laughter on the other end of the line. The phone went dead and as soon as I put the receiver down myself I realised it was all a wind-up – and there was only one person capable of pulling such a stunt. Wally Downes.

I could have killed him. Not surprisingly, when I went into training the next day everyone had heard about me being taken in by Wally's prank and suddenly all the Liverpool jokes started. 'How's Bob Paisley then, Dave?' I tried to convince everyone that I knew it was a wind-up all along but they didn't buy it. I daren't repeat what I said to Wally at the time!

Any transfer talk was, however, the furthest thing from my mind as we prepared to make our latest assault on the Third Division. In previous years when the club had gone up to the Third – only to shoot straight back down like the proverbial yo-yo – we'd tried to operate a sweeper system, playing the ball out from the back and building our attacks from there. But such tactics clearly didn't work in the lower divisions so the educated stuff was abandoned and replaced by what became known as 'the Wimbledon way'. Amidst the hurly burly of the Third and Fourth Divisions the long ball became a vital part of our battle plan and it clearly paid dividends as we finished runners-up to book our place in the Second Division for the first time in the club's history. But, in our view, our methods weren't crude. In fact Harry put a lot of time and thought into the new approach, even to the point of employing a statistician to analyse our play in order to determine the most direct and profitable route to goal.

It certainly wasn't a case of simply hoofing the ball forward and hoping for the best (as some people would have you believe) because we did plan moves out. There was an art to playing that way and getting the best out of it. In order to do that, it required a lot of hard work during the week on the training ground. I'm convinced that's where we had the edge over a lot of teams and it showed after Christmas when our opponents were flagging but we were getting stronger and stronger. From lying in eighth place on Christmas Eve we only lost a handful of games between then and the end of the season and we won promotion with room to spare.

It was during this season that my long kicks were more in evidence because I introduced the 'dribble out' to my game, running the ball out of my area before pumping it down the channels. It was a tactic Hull 'keeper Tony Norman had employed against us early in the season and soon after Harry encouraged me to master the technique too. He asked me to stay behind after one particular training session and when he explained what he wanted me to do I though he was winding me up. I envisaged the lads to be watching from the changing-rooms having a good laugh at my expense as I ran the ball out of my area and cracked it deep into the other half of the field. But Harry was deadly serious and, sure enough, within a few weeks I was doing it in games. It paid off too and so became an important part of our play.

I was slightly nervous in the early days but it soon became second nature. It did almost back-fire on me, though, on one occasion towards the end of that season against Plymouth when, as no one came to close me down, I went on a run towards the half way line. When I eventually released the ball I mis-cued and struck a Plymouth player with the result that the ball went back over my head. I ran to retrieve it and tried a left-foot volley to safety but only succeeded in slicing the ball back towards my own goal. I ended up rushing into my box and diving on the ball with an opponent breathing down my neck. It was all exciting stuff for the crowd, although not quite as entertaining as a run I'd gone on at Walsall a few months before.

As a long ball came over the top of my defence towards me I could see two Walsall players converging on it so I rushed out of my box and proceeded to dribble the ball, from left foot to right, between the pair of them. As I did so another fella came at me from the right so I beat him as well and before I knew it I was five yards short of the half-way line with Harry doing his nut on the bench. With Walsall's back four pushing up towards half-way themselves I managed to keep my composure long enough to curl a magnificent pass with the outside of my right foot into Wally's path on the wing. Fancying myself a bit as a ball player I thought it was brilliant and after the game, which we ended up losing 4-0, Harry had a go at the other lads saying that our best outfield player on the day was me.

Defeats of that kind were few and far between and when we won the 'big one' at Sheffield United with a couple of games remaining promotion was virtually guaranteed. The crowd of almost 23,000 was one of the biggest I'd played in front of – it was also the first time I'd witnessed real crowd violence with United fans going on the rampage after the match. Police on horseback were called in to quell the disturbance and it was quite hairy as we made our way from Bramall Lane with bricks being thrown at the coach. The incidents were soon forgotten, however, as we clinched promotion at home to Gillingham two days' later – despite losing 3-1! As the final whistle blew I reached into my goal to pick up my bag thinking we had blown it but suddenly the fans, who had just heard the other results, came charging on to the field shouting, 'We've done it.'

The celebrations, which began there and then with the supporters ripping virtually all my kit off to keep as souvenirs, capped a great season which had also seen us enhance the club's giant-killing reputation with a two-leg win over Nottingham Forest in the Milk Cup. Having beaten Southend 6-5 on aggregate in the first round we took on Forest in front of the TV cameras and stuffed them 2-0. In the return at the City Ground we held them to a 1-1 draw and went through at a canter. Sadly, after beating Oldham in the third round, our Cup run came to a disappointing end at Rotherham. But we had served a warning to the rest of the country that Wimbledon meant business.

Having ended the season on a high, however, disappointment was just around the corner in the shape of Harry's sad departure to Crystal Palace. The first I knew about it was after the last game of the 1983-84 season when we were celebrating promotion in a London pub. All the lads were in typically high spirits and the booze was flowing, but for once Harry wasn't joining in the fun. At one stage I looked round and he was sitting in a corner with his head in his hands virtually crying in his beer. Although there had been nothing in the papers, and Harry himself hadn't said anything about leaving, I sensed that he was on his way out. I went over and put it to him that he was going to another club, but he wouldn't admit it so Stewart Evans and I (the two biggest blokes in the club) threatened to beat him up if he went and it was left at that. It wasn't until a while later that Harry called us into the ground to tell us he really was leaving to go to Crystal Palace.

Nobody wanted to believe it and we all sat with our heads bowed thinking it was the end of the world. Some of us had tears in our eyes and as Harry said his farewells you could tell that he was filling up too. Harry wasn't just a manager; he was like a father to us and it felt as though our Dad was leaving home, that's how much we thought of him and how much we were going to miss him. From being on a high after winning promotion we were on the floor, but before the full effects of Harry's departure had sunk in he was back at the club. His reign as Palace boss lasted two days and needless to say when he did return he came in for a lot of stick. We all knew he just couldn't bear to leave us.

The funny thing is that, on the eve of Harry's exit, he'd told me that Coventry boss Bobby Gould had made an inquiry about me . . . for the second time. But as Harry was technically no longer in charge at the time of the conversation he'd told Bobby that he had better discuss the matter with the new manager when he came in. As it turned out the 'new boss' was Harry who, somewhat inevitably, never mentioned Coventry or Bobby Gould to me again. Funny that. He felt that I needed to gain some experience of life in the Second Division before trying to make my mark in the First. Now where had I heard that before? I suppose he was right . . . as always. Unlike the previous summer, when I'd set my heart on a move to Stoke, I didn't really want to leave and I was more than happy to stay and hopefully help the club continue our remarkable journey through the divisions to the top flight.

Our first season in Division Two began promisingly enough with a 2-2 draw at home to one of the promotion favourites, Manchester City. But two successive defeats against Birmingham (2-4) and Oxford (1-3) soon brought us down to earth and made us realise that getting into the First Division was going to be no cakewalk. By Wimbledon's standards the season was something of a non-event, the majority of it being spent in mid-table, and we were never in a position to challenge for promotion. From November onwards we seemed to be glued to the unlucky 13th spot and it was only when we beat Cardiff in the final game of the season that we leapt a massive one place to 12th! We were far too inconsistent – winning a couple here, losing a few there – and after winning promotion two years running we were disappointed with our final position. But at least we had never been in any danger of being relegated, as many people had predicted when we were promoted from the Third Division, and the season was seen as a period of re-adjustment and consolidation. Our promotion charge would come next season, we decided.

There had been a few comings and goings and the team which was to take everyone by surprise over the next few years was starting to take shape. People like Lawrie Sanchez, Dennis Wise, Andy Thorn, Brian Gayle and Carlton Fairweather were all relative newcomers to the side and it was understandable that they would take time to settle in. The foundations which had been laid in previous seasons were reinforced and the club was now in a position to build on the success we'd already enjoyed. The signs were there when we put together a decent run in the FA Cup and, while we struggled to find our true form in the League, collecting the scalp of Nottingham Forest (for the second successive season) gave us hope for the future. We did superbly to hold them to a goalless draw at the City Ground – my most memorable match for Wimbledon so far – and beat them 1-0 in the replay. Apart from the Cup run, which ended with a 5-1 defeat at West Ham in a fifth round replay, one of the most memorable moments of the season came during a 3-2 win against our arch-rivals Portsmouth in October.

It all started when Corky scored one of our three goals and collided with Pompey 'keeper Alan Knight in the process. My opposite number was quite badly hurt and, as Portsmouth took the kick-off, he still looked in a bit of trouble. The funny thing was that from the re-start Portsmouth, under pressure from our forwards, were forced back towards their own goal and I watched in amazement as Noel Blake hit a back pass straight past his keeper who was still busy rubbing his injured leg. With Knight stranded, the ball rolled into the net for a remarkable own goal scored without a Wimbledon player touching it after the kick-off. So, with just one touch of the ball, we had scored two goals. To complete an amazing afternoon I saved a Kevin Dillon penalty to secure the points – and was rewarded with a right hook straight to my jaw! It came from one of the many Portsmouth fans who invaded the pitch at the end. As they ran past me my first thought was to retrieve my glove bag – which had about £80 worth of gear in it – from the back of the net. As I made my way back I was given an almight punch in the face by some brave soul (probably a four foot midget for all I know) who took me completely by surprise. When I eventually got back into the dressing-room and told the lads what had happened everyone burst out laughing. I suppose I was wrong to expect sympathy. At least Portsmouth boss Alan Ball issued a public apology on behalf of the 'mindless' few who had marred a good game of football.

From a personal point of view the 1984-85 season was a disappointing one because we conceded 75 goals in the League alone – four more than we actually scored. It was an area in which we needed to tighten up and when we began our second season in Division Two with a couple of clean sheets against Middlesbrough and Leeds we seemed to have got the formula right. We conceded just four goals in our opening seven League games – all four coming in one match at Sheffield United! – and that gave us the perfect start.

After the game at Elland Road in midweek Harry decided we would stay up in Yorkshire to prepare for the game at Bramall

Lane on the Saturday. A nice week away, we thought. Not a chance. Instead of booking us into an hotel Harry had arranged for us to stay at Harrogate Army barracks. It wasn't the first time he'd pulled a stunt like that (we often spent pre-season training with the army, tackling assault courses and the like) and he obviously felt that, in addition to improving our fitness, living rough for a few days was a good, character-building exercise. Mind you, after a painful experience Harry endured on a previous venture at barracks in Plymouth I'm surprised he was so keen to join in. On that occasion he was rushed off to hospital to have stitches in a head wound caused when he cracked his skull in a water-filled tunnel.

Most of the time, however, our experiences of army life were fun and if nothing else they cemented the team spirit amongst the lads. They also provided us with a welcome break from the traditional routine of a pro-footballer. Once, we were even sent on a night raid, kitted out in full army uniform and equipped with flares and thunder flashes. It was designed to be as realistic as possible and I must admit, at times, I found it quite nerve-racking – especially going through underground tunnels laid with booby traps at midnight. We were warned by the professionals that if a thunder flash went off in the tunnel it would probably deafen us for a few seconds. They also put the wind up us by insisting that when a flash goes off in such a confined space it causes a vacuum and can blow out any fillings that you might have in your teeth. To guard against it we were told to keep our mouths open if we heard the hiss of a flash about to go off. Whether they were just winding us up, and I suspect they were, I don't know but we all followed their instructions and must have looked a rare old sight stumbling around in dark tunnels with our mouths wide open. Good job it was dark! The stint at Harrogate, however, didn't exactly work in our favour because we lost our next match at Sheffield United 4-0. Perhaps if they had bombarded us with hand grenades instead of a football we might have been able to cope!

It was only a temporary set-back and we were soon back on course for promotion. From 11 January onwards, following a 2-1 reverse at Oldham, we went 16 games undefeated to finish

the season in the third promotion place. The pleasing thing
from my point of view was that I was made captain after the
Oldham game and, therefore, went through the rest of the
season without skippering a losing side.

We clinched our place in Division One for the first time in

*Actress June Whitfield catches her 'Greek God' in the all-together . . .
again!*

the club's history with a 1-0 win at Huddersfield (Sanch scoring the all important goal) and the champagne was flowing in the dressing-room afterwards when actress June Whitfield, one of our famous fans, came strolling in to offer her congratulations. She went round the room shaking everyone's hand before turning to me. The problem was that, as I was standing on the bench at the time without a stitch on, the nearest thing to her hand was . . . well I think you can guess what it was! We had a good laugh about the incident (at least I think that's what she was laughing about!) and we became good friends afterwards with June insisting on calling me her Greek god. Her interest in football grew from then on (far be it for me to suggest why) and she later became president of the supporters' club, a sign that she'd taken Wimbledon FC to her heart.

That couldn't be said of the majority of football followers, however, because we gained few friends for the so-called 'unacceptable' style which had taken us to the top. In fact our long-ball tactics, coupled with our somewhat abrasive approach, suddenly made Wimbledon FC public enemy number one – not that it worried us. We were playing to our strengths and our attitude was that, as long as it brought us results, we would continue with it. We felt we had introduced a touch of culture to our play, it wasn't just hump and hope, and in some respects we were trying to copy Liverpool. Whenever Harry wanted to illustrate how to play the long ball properly he would show us a video of the 'Mighty Reds' in action. By studying film of them we soon learned that a lot of their goals come from long, direct passes. The annoying thing was that when WE did it, it was 'crap' and yet when Liverpool did it, it was 'wonderful'.

Because we collected quite a few bookings and sendings off along the way our reputation as the so-called bad boys of English soccer began to grow. Yet, while we did run up too many disciplinary points and were punished by the FA on occasions as a result, we never considered ourselves to be a dirty side. We would always fight for every ball and we would always give 100 per cent but we were never told to stop teams playing by kicking them off the park. If you are giving 100 per cent for 90 minutes you expect to commit a few fouls but, in my view, we were never malicious. Hard but fair. It was our never-say-die attitude which made us so successful and there was no way we were going to change to suit everyone else. We were proud of our achievement, and rightly so, and we felt that any criticism of us was borne purely out of jealousy. Our record of going from the Southern League to the First Division in less than ten years was unprecedented and no one could take it away from us, or even tarnish it in any way with their cheap jibes.

Having threatened to leave Wimbledon a couple of years before because I wanted to play First Division football I was thrilled that I was now going to fulfil that ambition with the club which had given me my big break in the game. At one time I never imagined that it would be possible to do that with the Dons but I didn't mind being proved wrong. At 27 I was something of a late entrant to the top flight but for me the wait had been worthwhile. I'd got there the hard way and it meant more to me than I could ever describe. We had got what we deserved and even if the rest of the football world disagreed we didn't care because we had all set out with an ambition and we'd achieved it. Nothing else mattered. The important thing was that, from the beginning of the 1986-87 season, we would be going to places like Old Trafford and Anfield instead of Gay Meadow or Brunton Park. To me that said it all and I couldn't wait for the season to start.

We were all confident that we could hold our own in the top flight although, almost inevitably, we were written off as relegation certainties by sections of the media who were now committed Wimbledon haters. Our reputation had gone before us and it was something we had to learn to live with. By continually making us out to be villains or second-class citizens all the knockers and the doubters had done was to stoke the fire in the Wimbledon bellies even more and make us even more obstinate and resolute. All the lads at the club had worked hard to put Wimbledon on the map, probably a lot harder than any other players in the First Division at the time, and people were wrong to suggest we shouldn't be there. We weren't deterred by the criticism though and neither were we worried about what the top flight had in store for us or the so-called pressures it would bring. As my old mate Wally Downes once said, 'Pressure isn't about playing the likes of Liverpool, pressure is about being second from the bottom of the Third Division with only nine men available on a Thursday.' He was absolutely right because, after what we'd all been through together over the years, we were able to handle anything the First Division and its soccer giants could throw at us. Our attitude was that we were there on merit and we were there to stay.

And we didn't see the need to change our style of play either. It had served us well over the years, as it had done Watford and Sheffield Wednesday, and as far as we were concerned it would be business as usual. We felt we were more than capable of achieving a mid-table position, at least, and the fact that most people thought we would get our come-uppance took any pressure that there might have been off us. We were the underdogs in virtually every game we played and that suited us down to the ground.

We took our First Division bow at Maine Road, a stadium which was familiar to us, having played Manchester City a couple of seasons before in the Second Division. During the build-up to the game the TV cameras had been following us everywhere and on the Friday night they had filmed us preparing for the big day at our team hotel in Manchester. It must have made interesting viewing as we sat down for our evening meal at tables placed in the middle of the dance floor of the hotel disco with a party going on around us. The hotel must have double-booked us with a social gathering of some description and the dance floor was the only space they had left to put our dinner tables. With disco lights flashing all around us and party streamers hanging over the tables it must have looked as though we weren't taking our first match very seriously. Heaven knows what our wives and girlfriends must have thought, when they saw us on screen apparently living it up in a Manchester disco because we'd always assured them that overnight stays in hotels were low-key and boring.

As it turned out we lost our opening game 3-1, although the

defeat had nothing to do with our preparations. In fact we went 1-0 up just after half-time, courtesy of a 30-yard free-kick by Andy Thorn, and looked as though we would kick-off our First Division careers with a famous victory. Unfortunately we didn't bank on City bringing on a super sub in the shape of Paul Simpson who tore our full-back John Kay to shreds to inspire a remarkable comeback. Within ten minutes of him coming on we were 3-1 down and we left the field completely shell-shocked. We learned a valuable lesson that day, however, and one which was to stand us in good stead for the rest of the season.

Apart from a mad, ten-minute spell we hadn't played that badly, but that didn't stop *Daily Star* reporter Ken Lawrence labelling us 'the worst team I have ever seen at Maine Road'. He also reckoned we were dead certs for relegation and so, on the Monday when his report appeared, Fash got on the phone to him to put him right on a few things. The call ended with Fash betting the writer a crate of champagne that we would stay in the First Division. It wasn't just in the *Star* that we were slaughtered, however, and we were all fuming about the Press we received.

Although we won our second match – at home to Villa – I conceded another two goals and was more than a little concerned about the start I'd made to my First Division career. So much so that I went in to see Harry to ask him where he thought I was going wrong. I had begun to doubt my own ability and wonder whether I'd got what it takes to play at the top level. In the opening two games our opponents had only had half-a-dozen attacks and they'd scored five goals, but Harry did his best to assure me that I wasn't completely to blame. Thankfully, after keeping clean sheets in the next three games, my confidence was fully restored and to everyone's surprise we were sitting pretty at the top of the First Division. We were only there for a week, but it was nice while it lasted and, following a 1-0 win at Watford, we had a few celebration drinks on the strength of it.

Our sensational start, however, must have gone to our heads because we managed just one point from our next six games and slumped to 14th place. People were quick to say that the bubble had burst, especially after Liverpool had dished out a 3-1 hammering at Plough Lane at the beginning of October. It was my first taste of the finishing power of Ian Rush and, as he sealed a comfortable Liverpool victory, I remember thinking how far we had to go to reach that standard. But we had learned another valuable lesson.

Because of injuries Harry was forced to chop and change the team around with the result that, towards the end of November, he gave a debut to a lad called Vince Jones. Vinny made an instant impact, scoring on his home debut in a 1-0 win over Manchester United and then notching again in successive victories against Chelsea and Sheffield Wednesday. 'Psycho', as he was nicknamed by the fans, had arrived. He added steel to the midfield and we looked a better balanced outfit with him doing his stuff 'in the mixer' – the crucial midfield area where most of the action is.

It was in a 4-0 win at Chelsea that we were involved in our first top flight punch-up, although the flare-up which comprised of 21 of the 22 players wasn't started by a Wimbledon player. It was provoked by Doug Rougvie's outrageous attack on me as I dived at his feet to smother the ball. I had possession when he suddenly started lashing out with his feet, kicking me time and time again in the chest like some kind of maniac. Even the referee was quoted after the game as saying he had never seen such an evil look on a player's face as Rougvie displayed that day. Such is the Wimbledon spirit ('all for one, one for all') it didn't take the lads long to pile in to protect me and let Rougvie know, quite politely of course, he was out of order. All the Chelsea players, barring 'keeper Eddie Niedzwiecki, steamed in as well and for a minute or so there was pandemonium in my penalty area. It was no great surprise when Rougvie, who had hit me on two other occasions earlier in the game, was sent off. He had been fired up from the start, that was blatantly obvious, but by that stage he had completely flipped and had to go.

That 4-0 win represented one of our best performances of the season, second only to a famous victory on our first ever visit to Anfield on 28 March 1987. Yet while the 2-1 triumph was memorable in itself the thing I remember most about the day was a sequence of events involving Carlton Fairweather and his amazing gold chain, a 24-inch monster which made him look like Mr T. We always warned him against wearing jewellery, as referees insist, but he never paid any attention and on this day he almost paid the penalty. During a Liverpool attack, the chain fell off and landed somewhere in our penalty area. As I screamed at our defence to push out, having cleared the ball, Carlton suddenly came running back to me and pleaded: 'Have a look for my chain will you? It's come off.' I couldn't believe my ears but I automatically began looking for it. Incredible really when you consider that in the heat of battle against the most dangerous attacking team in the land I was scouring my box for Carlton's blasted chain. I found it too. What with winning 2-1, thanks to goals by Nigel Winterburn and Alan Cork, it was quite an eventful game.

The fun continued in the dressing-room afterwards with us performing a celebration dance to the 'house music' sounds coming out of Vinny's ghetto blaster. It was also the occasion that Vinny made headline news by confronting Kenny Dalglish, who had scored an unbelievable goal, and threatening to 'rip off his head and s*** in the hole'. Hardly the sort of thing you say to one of the most respected figures in the game but that was typical of Vinny's over-exuberance and naivety. It was incidents like that which led to him getting the 'tough nut' reputation he'll probably have to live with for the rest of his career.

But, despite the fact that the aristocrats of English football had been turned over by the First Division's poor relations, Liverpool were gracious in defeat. Ronnie Moran and Ray Evans were particularly kind to our backroom staff, inviting them into the famous boot room for a drink or two after the game. More like seven if you'd seen the state of them when they rolled out. It was something the likes of Sid the kit man and Alan Gillett will never forget. Losing to us must have been a bitter pill for Kenny Dalglish and Co to swallow but the Liverpool boss refused to slag off our style of play, preferring instead the diplomatic approach by explaining to the Press that we had simply played to our strengths.

As the season went on it seemed that the only teams to criticise us and moan about our no-nonsense methods were sides we had beaten. And there were a few of them that season as we went on to finish in a commendable sixth place. In League terms at least we had excelled ourselves but, by the same token, we had let ourselves down in the FA Cup. Having reached the sixth round we froze against Spurs (we tried to match them in the fancy dan stakes instead of playing our normal game) and made a sad exit with Wembley beckoning. As part of our build-up to the game we'd been to Spain for a few days, as we had done before previous rounds, but the get-away-from-it-all plan backfired. I'm convinced it was because on this occasion we were taken to the lively resort of Torremolinos where there were too many distractions. Perhaps some players treated it too much as a holiday with the result that we weren't mentally prepared for such an important Cup game. Two late goals by Waddle and Hoddle confirmed Tottenham's superiority on the day and our Wembley dream lay in tatters.

There was even more disappointment to come at the end of the season when Harry announced he was leaving the club. Although he'd left once before to join Palace, only to return after two days, he meant it this time. He stage-managed his exit pretty well too, announcing his intention to quit a couple of days before Wally Downes' testimonial match at Plough Lane. It wasn't that he'd wanted to upstage Wally, he simply felt that by coinciding his departure with that game it would attract a bigger crowd to the ground for Wally's benefit. It was also a fitting way of saying goodbye and thank you to the hard core Wimbledon following. From what I could gather Harry wasn't happy with the new contract the club had offered him and, as he no longer saw eye-to-eye with Managing Director, Sam Hamman, the only option open to him was to leave. He felt he'd done as much as he could at Wimbledon and needed a new challenge. We understood his feelings but no one wanted him to go, least of all the fans who turned up at Wally's testimonial match parading banners to the effect of 'Harry stay . . .

Hamman go'. As far as Harry was concerned, however, there was no turning back.

The news didn't produce the shock waves that his decision to go to Palace had done a couple of years before but it was still disappointing to part company with the man many of us had grown up with. He was a successful young manager with a growing reputation in the game and it was inevitable he would want to go on to bigger and better things at another club at some time. That time had arrived and it signalled the end of a glorious and memorable era. Having reached that stage it came as no real surprise when a crop of players, myself included, felt we had reached the end of the Wimbledon line too. Following Harry's departure unrest within the club grew and it was inevitable changes would take place. The underlying fear amongst the players concerned the appointment of Harry's successor and whether or not he would ring the changes himself as new managers invariably did. Some of us didn't want to stick around to find out.

CHAPTER FIVE

All the Way to Wembley

It was while I was away enjoying a well-earned summer break that the news was released of Harry's replacement. Bobby Gould was the man who had agreed to undertake what many saw as a 'mission impossible' replacing the manager who in our eyes was Mr Wimbledon. It couldn't have been an easy decision to make and I remember Bob remarking at the time that he had taken on the most difficult task in English football – replacing Harry Bassett. Having been associated with Bob as a player at Wimbledon for a short spell a good few years before, I considered the appointment an excellent one. Like Harry he was young, in managerial terms at least, with the type of personality which would enable him to step into the job with a good deal more comfort than may have been the case with other candidates. He also knew something about the club and the way Wimbledon FC operated.

Almost as soon as he took over he announced his intention to run the club along similar lines to those which Harry had followed and, when asked if he was planning to make sweeping changes, it was good to hear him say: 'Why should I meddle with a successful formula?' In fact one of his few stipulations when he took over was that we referred to him either as Bob, boss or gaffer and not 'Morocco Mole' as he'd been nicknamed as a player at Plough Lane because of his friendship with Harry. Bob's 'business as usual' pledge didn't, however, stop the likes of Glyn Hodges, Nigel Winterburn and Kevin Gage (all out of contract) seeking a move but there wasn't the mass exodus many had predicted.

For my own part I was still slightly unsettled, not because I felt the club had reached the end of the road with Harry on his way to Watford, but because, like my old boss, I felt the need for a fresh challenge. I'd been at the club a long time and considered that a transfer to a bigger outfit was what I needed to keep my career moving in the right direction. That's why, in only my second meeting with Bob, I told him I wanted a move (I didn't have the heart to tell him during our first meeting). I emphasised that my decision had nothing to do with his appointment as manager and that I would have felt the same whoever was in charge. My problem was that I still had two years of my contract to run and, while Bob understood my predicament, he insisted that he wanted me to stay. As a goalkeeper and a captain he saw me as a key figure in his team. Having tried to sign me twice in the past – as assistant to Geoff Hurst at Chelsea and later as manager of Coventry – he told me:'I've had to come to Wimbledon to get you and now I've got you I don't want to let you go.' He even offered to extend my two year contract to the three years that he had committed himself to the club and I was flattered, not to mention reassured, by his gesture. Although I declined the offer of an extended contract I agreed to stay on the understanding that he would keep me informed of any interest from other clubs. As things transpired during Bob's first season in charge I'm glad I decided to reaffirm my allegiance to the club.

In fairness to Bob he tackled the job superbly and, together with newly appointed coach Don Howe, he managed to maintain the atmosphere and team spirit on which Wimbledon thrived. He enjoyed a laugh and a joke as much as the next man. It may not have been quite the same as before, it could never be the same, but he had everyone pulling together and we all had respect for him and Don. Even Don, whom we had envisaged as a strict disciplinarian who ruled with a rod of iron, joined in the fun. He looked as though he was enjoying his new role and he appreciated the fact that all the players were willing to listen to, and learn from, him. He had a lot to offer and the same applied to Bob. They complemented each other well and operated as a team in much the same way as Harry and Alan Gillett had done in the past. It did take a while though for us to get Harry out of our system and for Bob to settle in but the lads did accept him and I can't think of one player who took offence to him or his methods of management. And he wasn't above coming to us and seeking our opinions or asking how we used to do certain things under the old régime. He had his own ideas and habits, just as his predecessor had, but he was flexible and we respected him for that too.

For a time, however, it couldn't have been easy for him because although Harry had gone, it was as though he was still there in spirit. There was no way the players could forget about him just like that and, as he was considered a close friend by most of the lads, we kept in touch with him on that basis. His name was forever cropping up in conversation either on the training field or in the dressing-room and even very early on I could sense that Bobby was getting sick and tired of having Harry's name rammed down his throat. It began to get to him and he must have felt that our preoccupation with Harry and the past was undermining his position as manager. He wanted us to come to terms with the fact that he was the boss and that Harry was history – and the sooner the better. There was one occasion when Bob, who was clearly fed up with hearing Harry's name, put a block on us talking to our old boss – about football at least. He didn't mind us socialising with him but he didn't want us discussing problems or grievances we might have. Maybe he was worried that if Harry sensed we were unhappy he might make a move for us. Bob didn't want the boat rocked so early on in his Wimbledon career.

By a strange quirk of fate his first League game in charge was against Harry's Watford at Vicarage Road and it was a weird feeling going out to try and put one over on our ex-boss. As it happened, we didn't. We lost 1-0. We still ended up going for a drink with Harry – and Elton John! – afterwards and, although Bob would no doubt have been pleased had we blanked Harry on the day, there was never a danger of that happening. He was still 'one of us'. There were times when Bob would refer to the 'ghost of Harry Bassett' and he must have wondered whether he would ever lay that ghost. The only way he could hope to achieve that would be to add his own chapter to the Wimbledon success story by leading us to one of the major honours. With the League title realistically out of his reach it was in the Cup competitions that his best chance lay.

By the start of the season he had everyone's mind right and the new Wimbledon was ready to take over from where the old Wimbledon had left off. Having done so well in our first year in Division One – we'd finished sixth in the League and reached the quarter-finals of the FA Cup – we were looking to build on that success and prove to the doubters that what we'd achieved during the 1986-87 season was no flash in the pan. We were never going to challenge the likes of Liverpool and Everton for the Championship so, although we were in the top six by the time third round day came around in January, our sights were well and truly set on the FA Cup. For so many years Wimbledon had been the underdogs in the competition, potential giant-killers but with no hope of going all the way. Well, now it was different. Because we'd reached the sixth round the previous season and started to build a reputation as a difficult team to beat, we were being taken seriously for the first time. We felt we should have gone further in the competition the previous season but we really let ourselves down against Spurs in the quarters. And I felt responsible for the 2-0 defeat as anyone after being beaten at the near post by a Chris Waddle shot and from about 30 yards by a Glenn Hoddle screamer. On the big day we froze but we were determined the same wouldn't happen this season.

We kicked off the competition against West Brom brimming with confidence after winning five League games on the trot over the Christmas period. Wimbledon, traditionally, tended to come on strong after the Christmas break and there are two possible explanations for it. The first is that while other teams are still running off the turkey and the booze, Wimbledon, because we liked a drink all year round, weren't so affected by the over-indulgence. People claimed we were so accustomed to the drink that a little more at Christmas made no difference. I preferred to think that it was down to the fact we were working harder in training than other teams who perhaps had let their training schedule slip as the season wore on. Harry had always encouraged us to keep doing the runs and the shuttles right through the winter, convinced we would be stronger than our rivals over 90 minutes on the heavy pitches. Invariably he was right and Bobby Gould carried on the good work with tremendous success.

So with five wins out of five leading up to the third round, and a home tie against a Second Division club in prospect, we could see no problems in disposing of West Brom. That's exactly how things turned out in the end, although we didn't start the game against Albion too well. We allowed them a few chances early on and it wasn't until Fash put us ahead before half time that we started to make them suffer. With the wind behind us in the second half there was no stopping us and Dennis Wise put us 2-0 up with an absolute cracker from 30 yards. Mind you he almost broke his leg in the process when he made contact with his marker on the follow through. He was on the ground writhing in agony as the ball screamed into the top corner and he was forced to go off shortly afterwards. Robbie Turner came on as sub for Wisey and promptly scored his first competitive goal for the club. Carlton Fairweather made the score 4-0 and although Andy Thorn put an own goal past me late on it was a convincing win and our confidence was stronger than ever.

The draw for the fourth round, however, rocked us back on our heels because we were handed a potentially dangerous visit to Mansfield. Although they were a Third Division side we knew from our own experiences of the past how teams like that relish the prospect of dumping a First Division side on the seat of their pants. We'd done it to a few clubs in our time and suddenly there was a danger that the roles could be reversed and we could be on the receiving end of a giant-killing. The day itself didn't start too well for us because on the way to the ground our coach was caught up in a wicked traffic jam and there was a danger that Bobby and I wouldn't get the team sheet into the referee on time. For League matches the line-up has to be presented to the ref at two-fifteen and we assumed the same applied to Cup matches. When the coach arrived at the ground Gouldy and I leapt off and got to the referee's dressing-room with about two minutes to spare only to be told that the team sheet didn't have to be in until two-thirty!

The conditions on the day were lousy and a gale-force wind, combined with a boggy pitch, threatened to make the game a lottery. Mansfield came at us early on as we expected but we rode the storm and Corky put us ahead before half-time with a classic header. With the wind assisting us in the second half I was able to put my long kicks to good use and it was from one Beasant boomer that Terry Phelan stole forward to make it 2-0. It was then that we made the fatal mistake of believing the game was won and we allowed them back into the match with some sloppy defensive play. Brian Gayle under-hit a back pass to me and as I came rushing out to clear the danger, the ball hit a bobble and I ended up taking an almighty swipe at nothing but thin air. I was in no-man's-land as Kevin Kent walked the ball in. Suddenly, from being in complete command, we were up against it. The lads gave me a bit of stick afterwards, claiming that a field mouse must have popped up and flicked the ball over my foot, but I simply blamed the pitch. Mansfield, now with a second wind, started to make us look a bit silly and in the closing stages we conceded a penalty which might well have signalled the end of our Cup run.

The strange thing was that, on the morning of the game, we had been watching TV clips of Mansfield's penalty shoot-out in the Freight Rover Trophy final the previous year. The winning penalty was taken by a left-footed player who blasted his spot-kick to the keeper's left and, although it didn't register at the time, when I came face to face with the same fella (at least I thought it was the same player) in the afternoon I sensed he would put his shot to my left. Sure enough he did and I managed to hang on to the ball and so give us a vital victory. Afterwards I was talking to the Press about my save and I nonchalantly boasted about the fact that I'd seen the fella take a penalty at Wembley in the Freight Rover and knew which side he was going to put it. In the papers the next day, however, the guy who took the penalty at Mansfield said: 'Beasant did well to see me in the final at Wembley because I wasn't even playing.' That took the wind out of my sails, I can tell you. But the important thing was that we'd overcome a difficult obstacle. In fact Mansfield probably provided us with our biggest scare en route to Wembley and we needed a bit of luck to see them off at the first attempt.

In the next round we were paired with Newcastle and, even before a ball was kicked, we felt that if we could get a result at St James' Park we would go all the way to Wembley. This was the big one as far as we were concerned and we were really fired up for what was labelled a 'grudge match' because of what had gone on between Vinny and Paul Gascoigne in a League match at Plough Lane a few weeks before. Prior to that game Bobby Gould had decided that for once we would change our style to counteract Gazza, and Vinny was earmarked to do a man-to-man marking job on the Newcastle danger man. As it turned out it was more a man-to-manhood marking job that Vinny did – as the pictures in the papers the next day clearly illustrated. But, from the team's point of view Vinny had done a great job because Gazza hardly had a kick. The ironic thing was that in the days leading up to the League clash, after Bobby had outlined the task he wanted Vinny to do, we had a practice match to give Vinny some experience of a man-to-man job. He was told to mark Andy Clement out of the game but he had a nightmare and we all thought at the time, 'How the hell's he going to cope with Gazza?' As it turned out he marked Gazza out of the match but, because of the infamous 'nutcracker' incident, he never got the credit he deserved. To both players' credit they gave each other a hug after the game and even exchanged crazy gifts; Vinny sending Gazza a toilet brush and Gazza sending Vinny a red rose. After that they were the best of mates and, although the Newcastle fans thought otherwise, there was never any danger of the two players – or the two teams come to that – using the re-match in the Cup to settle the scores.

It was only to be expected that on the day Vinny would get merciless stick from the Newcastle fans and, sure enough, he was booed virtually every time he went near the ball. There were also anti-Vinny banners all round the ground proclaiming things like 'Vinny bites yer nuts' and 'Vinny Jones reaches the parts other players cannot reach'. It must have been a nerve-racking weekend for Vinny because before we'd even arrived in Newcastle there were rumours that the fans were out to get him. Some were expected to turn up at the train station to greet him so we were given a police escort to the hotel and a guard was even posted at the door of the hotel to prevent unwelcome visitors coming in. An example of how tight security was emerged later when a former Wimbledon mate of mine Mick Smith, who was then living in Sunderland, had apparently telephoned the hotel and asked to speak to me, only to be told that the Wimbledon players were not staying there. He only succeeded in getting through to me when his wife phoned the hotel later saying she was my wife. It was a whole new ball game for us and the police were clearly taking seriously the threats some supporters had made to put the frighteners on Vinny. It takes a lot to scare Vinny and while I wouldn't say he was unduly worried by what was going on he was quiet, fairly subdued by Vinny Jones' standards in the build-up to the match.

But I think he was probably just thinking about the importance of the job he had to do the next day. After all it was a vital match for us. Once again he marked Gazza out of the game and I later learned from Geordie fans, and Willie McFaul, that after his confrontations with Vinny, Gazza never turned it on for Newcastle again. He was completely out of it. It was something totally new to Gazza and the experience of being shadowed by Vinny – not to mention some of the things our man was probably saying to him during the game – had frightened the life out of him.

Gazza certainly wasn't the influential player we were led

to believe he would be. Without him firing on all cylinders Newcastle were never much of a threat and when Terry Gibson gave us a first-half lead with a near post header it was no more than we deserved. The goal certainly took the sting out of the home crowd who had been quite vociferous in their support for Newcastle up until that point. In fact they started to turn against their team after that and at one point even applauded Vinny when he went close with a cracking drive from all of 25 yards.

You could sense the frustration creeping into Newcastle's play at the time and Mirandinha in particular started to lose his rag as things went against him. Apparently he had been saying in the papers all week how it was his dream to play in a Wembley Cup final and he was clearly well hyped up on the day. But he wasn't channelling his aggression and enthusiasm in the right way and the more we kept catching him offside the more his frustration and anger began to show. Our lads at the back could tell he was losing his cool so they kept winding him up to make him feel even worse. When Brian Gayle put us 2-0 up in the second half with a header we looked home and dry but, just as we'd let Mansfield off the hook in the last round, we did the same to Newcastle. Gazza, with his only real contribution in the game, took a great corner and Neil McDonald scored from three yards out. Suddenly the Geordie fans were back on song and we were up against it. But before they'd even looked like getting an equaliser Fash restored our two-goal cushion with a cracking left-foot volley following a free kick I'd taken just inside our own half. From then on we set out to kill the game, dispiriting Newcastle with possession football – or perhaps time-wasting would be a more accurate description.

Our tactics served to frustrate Mirandinha more than most. What annoyed me most about his behaviour was the way he kept spitting at Andy Thorn because in my book that sort of thing is totally unacceptable from a fellow professional. Every time the Brazilian ran past Thorny, Andy had to wipe his face clean. Later on in the game, when I tapped the ball away from Mirandinha as he tried to take a quick free kick, he went to spit in my face too. He was standing less than a yard away from me at the time but it missed and went over my shoulder. As he'd had a nightmare in front of goal that day I went up to him and, in my best English said: 'That sums you up. You're so crap you can't even spit in my face from two feet.' After that the lads just kept winding him up and, by the end of the match, he'd lost his rag completely.

As we walked off the pitch delighted with our 3-1 win Mirandinha, clearly upset because his Wembley dream had died, kicked me up the backside and then ran off down the tunnel. At the time I didn't know who had done it but some of the Wimbledon lads saw him do it and weren't too happy with him (to put it mildly). At first I thought it was a supporter who'd kicked me but when I saw some of our lads chasing Mirandinha down the tunnel I realised it must have been him. Terry Gibson was in hot pursuit and looking as though he could kill, so I grabbed hold of him and tried to calm everyone down. A few of the Newcastle lads helped quell the trouble as well and they all admitted that the Brazilian was bang out of order. There were crazy scenes in the tunnel and only thanks to the sensible attitude of the referee and certain players a potential punch-up was averted. After the game he came into the dressing-room with his interpreter Jimmy Wallace, apologised for what he had done and everything was forgotten about.

Needless to say the celebrations went on long into the night as we enjoyed a boozy trip back to London thinking to ourselves, 'Wembley here we come.' Even Corky, 'Mr. Depressive' as we called him, managed to raise a smile. He wasn't a 90-minute man any more and as he didn't start the game he probably felt a bit left out of it.

But he was back in the starting line-up for the next round – at home to Watford. At the time the draw was made our former boss Harry Bassett had just been sacked by Watford and I went on record in the Press as saying I'd like to beat them for Harry. I felt Watford hadn't given him a fair crack of the whip and their players hadn't given their all for him. Unfortunately the story landed me in hot water with Bobby Gould and Don Howe who had a go at me about the comments

I'd made, claiming that all I'd achieved was to fire the Watford players up and give them an extra incentive to beat us. They were probably right and I accepted my ticking off like a man – I went home and cried! Seriously though, by that stage not even a fired up Watford side was going to stop us progressing to the semi-finals for the first time in the club's history.

A week or two before the Cup clash we played Watford in the League and they beat us 2-1, so it seemed my comments had revved them up but, with home advantage in the quarter-finals, I was confident we would turn them over. During the build-up I chose to maintain a low profile and keep my thoughts to myself, preferring instead to let the team do the talking for me on the day. And they didn't let me down . . . in the end. We had a couple of scares along the way, not least when Brian Gayle was sent off just before half-time with us already 1-0 down to a Malcolm Allen goal. He seemed to lash out at someone over by the touchline right in front of the referee and the linesman. He didn't have a hope of staying on and to lose a man with half the match remaining was the last thing we needed. Psychologically the sending off was a massive boost for Watford and a demoralising blow for us. In boxing terms we were on the ropes and praying for the bell which thankfully came a couple of minutes later in the form of the half-time whistle. If we had had to play on for much longer we could have been out for the count but the interval gave us a chance to regroup and set out a plan of action for the second half.

The half-time break was the turning point in the game as far as I was concerned because Watford must have come out thinking that they'd won it while we realised a super-human effort was needed to get us out of the mess Brian had dumped us in. Needless to say Bobby Gould wasn't best pleased with Brian for his complete lack of discipline but rather than lay into him Gouldy put all his efforts into reorganising the troops and geeing everyone up. He and Don Howe did a brilliant job during that half-time break when they decided to drag Corky off and put Eric Young, a big centre-half, on in his place. It proved to be a master stroke because, although Eric was sent on to give us steel at the back, he also managed to head the equalising goal straight after the interval with virtually his first touch of the ball.

The goal gave us just the boost we needed and I remember thinking there and then that, even with ten men, we could go on and win it. We were fired up and Watford didn't know how to cope. When the odds are stacked against us there's no better fighting team in the country than Wimbledon and everyone seemed to raise their game 20 per cent to make up for the loss of a man while Watford were probably resting on their laurels. Instead of playing against ten men it must have seemed like they were up against 12 because we had players flying all over the place. There have been numerous games in the past when a ten-man team has overcome an obvious disadvantage to triumph against the odds. Look what Manchester United did to Everton in the 1985 FA Cup final after they'd had Kevin Moran sent off.

Once Eric had pulled us level we were all over them and sure enough Fash, with a typical piece of aggression and super cool finishing, kept us on course for Wembley with a great winner. Even after that goal, however, it wasn't just a case of us hanging on and we played out the game in style, getting the victory our courageous second-half performance deserved.

It was ironic that Brian's sending off had turned the game for us and was really a blessing in disguise because it meant we had to raise our game. It must have been difficult for him to celebrate what was a famous victory because we'd done it without him and the management left him in no doubt that he'd let the side down. As it turned out he didn't make another appearance for us in the competition and, therefore, missed out on all the Wembley glory and the Cup winners' medal which went with it. Shortly after the final he was sold to Manchester City so it was a sad end to his Wimbledon career. It must have been awful for him throughout the remainder of the Cup run because, having been involved in the first four rounds of the competition, he was suddenly on the outside looking in as the twin towers of Wembley loomed ever closer. For the rest of us though there was just one thing on our minds – an FA Cup semi-final clash with Luton at White Hart Lane.

Of the teams left in the competition – Luton, Forest and Liverpool – we were keen to avoid 'the big two' so the draw was ideal for us. We were even more delighted to learn that the game was to be played at White Hart Lane – a lucky ground for us in the past. Being a clash between two London clubs it was always a toss-up between Highbury and White Hart Lane for the venue. As we'd got a pretty good record in League games at Spurs but hadn't done so well at Highbury it was a great boost to us when the venue was announced. Even before a ball was kicked we felt we were one up, psychologically if not in real terms. But, for all our confidence and optimism, we tried not to get too carried away and our build-up to the game was relatively low-key. Well at least it was for the other lads.

For me the days leading up to the semis were arguably the most dramatic, the most exciting of my life. Sandra was due to give birth to a son at any moment, in fact she should have had Sam the week before the Luton match, but only began having labour pains on the Thursday prior to the big game. I took her into hospital at about 11 p.m. and, as there wasn't much I

One for the family album. Proud parents Dave and Sandra with sons Sam (left) and Nicky.

could do, I grabbed a pillow and went to sleep on the hospital floor, explaining to the nurses that I'd got an important game on the Saturday. I must have dozed off solid because the next thing I knew I was being shaken by a nurse telling me Sandra was about to give birth. Sam was eventually born just before three a.m. and I didn't get home to bed until about five. I woke up about nine o'clock feeling pretty shattered so I rang Bob at the ground to explain what had happened and ask if I could have a couple more hours in bed. He agreed and simply told me to report for a spot of training in the afternoon when he would check that I was feeling okay and in good physical condition for the game. In actual fact I felt fine, a little bit tired perhaps, but the good thing about it all was that I hadn't had time to get nervous about the game because my mind had been on other matters. By then the story had broke in the Press that I'd been up all night with Sandra and failed to report for training so, expecting the phone to be red hot, I took it off the hook when I got home and retired to bed at about eight p.m. I had a great night's sleep and didn't stir until ten the next morning by which time I was fully refreshed and ready for action.

Naturally I was on something of a high by now. Having had time to think about the semis, I was determined to make it a double celebration by getting to Wembley for Sandra and the baby. For the rest of the players, however, it was very much business as usual as regards the build-up and, as was the norm for away games in London, we all made our own way to Tottenham in cars rather than on a team coach. I can't imagine many other clubs allowing that to happen but that was Wimbledon FC for you . . . unique. One of the funny things to come out of it all was that Bob turned up at White Hart Lane in the club's mini-bus and for a start was refused entrance to the Tottenham car park. As the bus pulled up at the gate Gouldy, who was travelling with a driver and an apprentice assigned to carry the kit, explained that he was the manager of Wimbledon but an over-officious steward didn't believe him and said something like: 'If this is the team coach, where are the players?' The boss explained that we were travelling under our own steam and after a while he was let in. It could only happen to Wimbledon.

By the time we'd all assembled in the dressing-room the atmosphere had built up to something special and we began to realise that this was not 'just another game'. There were telegrams from family and friends everywhere and in the corner was a bunch of balloons Vinny had been given as good luck tokens from members of the Royal Ballet. In order to try and improve his image and prove to people that he had calmed down he'd made it known that he enjoyed a trip to the theatre – to see *The Nutcracker Suite* more than likely! Also in the dressing-room Bob had pinned up a newspaper article in which former player and manager Johnny Giles had slagged us off something chronic. He criticised our style of play and the essence of his message was 'I hope that, for the sake of football, Luton win because Wimbledon shouldn't be allowed to go to Wembley.' All the story achieved was to fire us up even more and Bobby simply pointed to the article and said: 'There's your team talk.' Nothing else really needed to be said.

Although the attendance at White Hart Lane was one of the smallest attracted to a semi-final for years the atmosphere when we walked out was still electric. But funnily enough, although it was the biggest game Wimbledon had ever played, we weren't at all nervous. That could hardly have been the case for Luton 'keeper Andy Dibble who was playing his first game for ages because of an injury to Les Sealey, so our pre-match plan was to put him under as much pressure as possible. In the first half we had three glorious chances, two of them one-on-one with the keeper, but all credit to Dibble who pulled off good saves on each occasion. When we went in at half-time with the score standing at 0-0 we were wondering whether it was going to be our day because we'd had the chances but had failed to make the most of them. When Mick Harford put Luton 1-0 up early in the second half our worst fears were in danger of being realised and at the time I felt we'd blown it.

I should have known better than to write our lads off, though, because in a situation like that there are no better ten players in the country to have in front of you. And true

Wimbledon's goal hero Dennis Wise gets a lift from big Dave as the two celebrate the Dons' FA Cup semi-final success over Luton.

to the fighting form Wimbledon had become renowned for we battled our way back into the game and received our reward when the ref awarded us a penalty when Dibble brought down Terry Gibson. John Fashanu stepped up to take it and with all the nonchalance and arrogance we'd come to expect from 'Fash

85

the Flash' he stroked the ball calmly home. I think he only took one stride before making contact and even looking at it on the video later the casualness he displayed almost gave me a heart attack. It wasn't a well-struck penalty and had Dibble gone the right way he would have had to wait for the ball to reach him. But the important thing was that we were level and from then on it would have taken a herd of elephants to stop us getting to Wembley. Sure enough, Wisey popped up to score the winner with a two-footed dive from about a yard out. It wasn't the best goal that's ever sent a team into the FA Cup final but what the hell? We were there.

The celebrations which greeted that goal were incredible and it still makes me smile to think of Bob, amidst all the euphoria, desperately trying to calm players down because we still had ten minutes left to hang on. Hang on we did and once that final whistle went all hell was let loose. The scenes of celebration and jubilation at White Hart Lane were even more outrageous than those which were to follow at Wembley. But while I shared a few glasses of champagne with the lads afterwards, courtesy of chairman Stanley Reid, I didn't go out on the town with the rest of them. Instead, Lawrie Sanchez and myself went back to my house to wet the new baby's head. Away from the euphoric scenes at Tottenham it gave us a chance to take in all that had happened and to think about the realisation of a dream every player harbours – to play in an FA Cup final at Wembley. The feeling of elation and ultimate satisfaction defies description and having been at the club so long and shared so many magical moments with so many fantastic people it was an occasion to cherish.

CHAPTER SIX

The Crazy Gang

From the day I joined Wimbledon as a naive teenager to the day I left, life at Plough Lane was one long feast of fun. With a cracking bloke like Harry Bassett in charge for the majority of the time I was there, how could it have been anything else? Of course it was hard work too and everyone knew that results on the field were the single most important thing. But Harry always made sure there was plenty of time for a laugh and a joke – and not just among a select few. The Crazy Gang, as we were christened in the Press, was made up of a handful of the club's characters (the 'Super Dons' as we called ourselves) but everyone on the staff at Wimbledon shared in the good times . . . from the chairman down to the youngest apprentice. That was the spirit of Wimbledon FC and the base on which the club was built.

The foundations for the success we enjoyed along the way, and the family atmosphere which has made the club so special, had already been laid by the time I joined Wimbledon. And a lot of the credit, in fact the majority of it, was down to one man – Harry Bassett. He was Mr Wimbledon and anyone who had the privilege of working with him during his time as player, assistant manager and boss has nothing but praise and respect for the bloke. It was Harry who was instrumental in signing me and it was him, as much as anyone, who was responsible for me enjoying nine great years on the Plough Lane payroll. He liked a laugh and a joke as much as the next fella and as assistant to Dario Gradi in the early days he even overstepped the mark himself on occasions.

Sometimes he knew when to end the joke and sometimes he didn't, wanting to take it to the limit. More often than not the joke was on him, like the time when we went on a cross country run with Harry resplendent in his bright yellow sweat top. It wasn't bright yellow for long though because half-way round we jumped him and rolled him in the mud. He was in a right state and he started to panic because he wasn't sure how he was going to explain this one away to the boss. Then there was the time when the players mugged him during a train journey back from a game in the north and prevented him getting off at his Watford Junction destination. We also pulled his shoes off and threw them out of the window of the train so he had to make his way back from Kings Cross to Watford without anything on his feet. He took it all in good part though.

In training we knew when it was time to buckle down and graft but we were always willing to take up the first opportunity to have some fun. Even the managing director Sam Hamman would join in the frivolities and that was typical of the way the club was run. I can still conjure up pictures of him slip-sliding his way on to the muddy training pitch wearing his suit and leather shoes to have a kick-about with the lads. He loved nothing more than having a few shots at me and he used to say: 'I'll put £100 into the players pool if I can't score more than three penalties out of ten past you.' He could hardly stand up let alone kick a ball in his leather shoes and there was never much danger of me losing the bet. Sam knew that too and really all he was doing was donating £100 into the pool. But he wanted to do it in his own way and we appreciated his generosity and the fact he wanted to get involved with the lads. He also used to challenge us to races with him starting on the half-way line and the rest of us having to run the length of the pitch. Because Wally Downes was one of the slowest members in the team he was allowed to start on the edge of the 18-yard box. The rest of us would pass the pair of them with ease but what Sam didn't realise was that while his back was turned we were creeping forward. He would be sliding all over the place as we ate up the ground in our boots, but it was all good fun and the sort of thing which maintained the friendly, family atmosphere we'd become accustomed to. It also meant we could have a few nights out at Sam's expense which was basically why he was doing it. He would take us out, wives and all, down to the Beer Kellar in the Strand or the Studio La Val Bon and he would be in the chair all night putting round after round of drinks on his American Express card. As we weren't on the greatest of wages playing in the lower divisions that was his treat and we all appreciated him for it. It was his way of bringing everyone together and for the most part it worked a treat.

It might sound corny but we were 'one big happy family' and there was always something going on, pranks being played or new phrases or sayings being bandied about that were unique to Wimbledon. Inside Plough Lane we had our own language, a vocabulary only people associated with the club would understand. A lot of the things we did and said probably wouldn't raise a smirk anywhere else but when you knew the crack it was hilarious. And that hilarity was virtually non-stop. Even now, in my darker moments, I'll sit down and think about some of the things we used to get up to and have a good old chuckle to myself. I'll treasure those memories, daft or otherwise, for as long as I live.

Neither will I forget some of the characters I met along the way. People like Steve Galliers, Steve Parsons and Gary Peters, all Wimbledon through and through, were game for a laugh in the early days. Gary, in particular, had a terrific sense of humour and was the sort of bloke who could laugh at himself too. We gave him an incredible amount of stick labelling him at one stage 'the worst right-back in the League' but he would happily go along with the joke. He'd even join in himself saying things like, 'I've cleared a few pigeons out of the main stand with my passes down the line since I've been here', or 'The pigeons have returned to the West Stand at Reading since I left the club.' If you weren't prepared to laugh at yourself at Wimbledon you were in big trouble and you'd get the mickey taken out of you even more.

But the fella who always cracked me up, and still does when I think about him today, was Wally Downes who, even as a youngster, ruled the roost at Wimbledon. He was usually at the centre of any high jinks that were going on and he was also the man assigned to break-in newcomers by seeing how they reacted to his incessant mickey-taking. When I first joined he would wind me up something chronic in training with remarks like 'Where d'you get him from, Harry?' or 'Send him back where you found him, Harry.' I squared up to him one day and we exchanged a series of meaningless threats but it was all in jest and I was soon accepted as one of the lads. Mind you, that didn't mean he had to stop winding me up. At one time before a cup match a newspaper approached him and asked if he could do a light-hearted run-down of his team-mates. Wally didn't need a second invitation to stitch up some of the lads and he proceeded to reveal secrets about everyone for which some of us were ridiculed for weeks after. In my case I was never allowed to forget something he wrote about me. Basically it was a dig about me never having any money on me when I went to training. I would only ever take as much as I needed for a drink and a snack afterwards, unlike Wally who would gorge himself stupid before going to work on his fruit and veg stall. The cash in my pocket normally amounted to very little and if anyone ever asked if I could lend them some money my reply was always: 'I can't, I've only got a quid on me.' Because of that he told the journalist that the wife wouldn't let me out of the house with any more than a quid adding: 'Lurch hasn't been married long and now the missus leaves him a quid behind the clock on the mantlepiece for his spending money every day.' I got stick from people for ages after that and couldn't even walk down the road without someone shouting, 'Have you got your quid from behind the clock, Dave?', or 'Do you want to borrow some money luv?' It was embarrassing for a while, but Wally had achieved what he'd set out to.

It was Wally who came up with most of the nicknames for

the lads and who christened me Lurch, presumably after the butler in *The Adams Family*. I can't see the resemblance myself. One of the funniest was the name he gave to Glyn Hodges . . . Le Head. Wally was forever going on about Hodgy's head being too big for his body and in the end Glyn got so paranoid about it that he asked for his head to be measured and compared with everyone else. He didn't want to carry the stigma of having the biggest head at the club so Wally got a boot lace and put it round his head to determine the size. Then, one by one, he would go round the other lads to find out if there was anyone at the club whose head wouldn't fit inside the hole Hodgy's had made. Everyone's head slipped through the lace a treat so Hodgy was stuck with his title. His only hope was that the club would sign someone with a bigger head and every time a new player joined the club Hodgy would take a long, hard look at him and then call to Wally 'get the boot lace out.' We'd be cracking up but the poor newcomer must have wondered what the hell was going on.

It must have been difficult for players coming into the club at that stage and trying to get to grips with Wally's sense of humour. I had enough trouble with him and I'd been there years. He had a wicked sense of fun and, at times, he could be quite cruel. Like the occasion when he rubbed Deep Heat into a cut on the head of our old physio (I can only remember him as 'Cod Head'), or the day he picked fun at former Bristol City 'keeper John Shaw. The player had unfortunately lost his hair through the disease alopecia, but that didn't deter Wally from taking the mickey out of him. Our resident lunatic considered it a good idea to run out on to the field with an old football bladder on his head making out that he was completely bald too. In the same game Wally went down injured (at least we thought he was injured) and when Derek French the physio came running on to treat him he leapt up and poured water all over Frenchy. The drenched French went mad and even threatened to resign later because he claimed he was 'fed up' with all the crazy antics that went on at the club. We ended up losing the game at Bristol 4-1 which was hardly surprising considering all the mucking about that went on.

No one was safe from Wally in those days, particularly yours truly, and he would pick on me all the time knowing that I would invariably rise to the bait. When things weren't going my way I would sometimes allow myself to slip into a mood and the lads would proceed to wind me up by saying, 'His lip's gone.' Wally had this ability to make my lip drop to the floor. On one occasion, though, he pushed me too far and he claims I came within a whisker of ending his career as I went in search of revenge.

It happened during training when Harry set up a one-on-one session for me with some of the lads, Wally included, attempting to take the ball round me. That was the plan anyway, but every time it was Wally's turn to take me on he would get within ten or 15 yards and then chip me, nutmeg me, curl the ball round me; anything but try to carry the ball round me as he was supposed to do. Every time he did it I would get more and more annoyed especially as, after each goal, he would ignore my pleas to co-operate by saying in his most sarcastic tone: 'Just get the ball out of the back of the net please, Dave.' By the fifth or sixth time I was fuming and ready to floor him. But Wally was relentless and as he was being egged on by the other lads – and a sniggering Harry Bassett on the sidelines – he just became more determined to wind me up. I called out to Harry, 'We are supposed to be doing one-on-one, aren't we?' But he just kept laughing. By then I was reaching breaking point and I shouted out to Wally that if he did get anywhere near me I would take him out in no uncertain manner. The next time, he came within five yards and just when I thought I had him he blasted the ball straight at me. I was livid, not to mention in a bit of pain, but all he could say was: 'Rub your leg, Dave, the pain'll soon go away.' That was it, I'd gone – and he knew he had me right on the end of his line. I threatened to do him again and accused him of not having the bottle to go round me.

The next time, however, he did try to take me on – 'try' being the operative word because as he went past me I took him out with a flying, two-footed tackle about knee height. I wasn't even looking at the ball, only at Wally. He went down like a sack of spuds and as he lay there writhing in agony I turned to Harry and said: 'I did warn him, Harry. He pushed me too far and now I've hurt him.' Suddenly the laughing and joking stopped and Harry came running over with a red face, worried that he'd let the wind-up go too far. Wally looked in a bad way but just as the boss called to Frenchy the physio he looked up at me and started sniggering. I was tempted to finish him off there and then. When I'd calmed down and we were back in the dressing-room Wally pointed to the spot where I'd caught him, explaining that it was inches above the place where he'd had a major cartilage operation when he was 16. At the time the op' specialists told him he would never play again and to this day he reckons that if I'd hit him a couple of inches lower I could have written his career off. All I could think to say at the time was: 'Well it serves you right, you shouldn't push me so far.' I don't recall him taking me to the edge again.

But that was the thing with Wally, he just never knew when to stop. He was the real joker in the pack, the vice-president of the Crazy Gang and second in line to Harry. He was brilliant for the club, the social secretary who was always organising functions left, right and centre. A trip down the dog track, the racecourse or even just down the pub; you name it, Wally organised it. With him around there was never a dull moment but some considered him to be a bad influence on the younger players around him. He was a bit outrageous at times but there was never any animosity involved in his pranks and because of his happy-go-lucky nature and overall charisma he could get away with things others couldn't. If anyone was going to over-step the mark or the bounds of lunacy it would be Wally. Similarly, if there were any pranks being played you could virtually guarantee that he would be at the bottom of it – quite literally when it came to the old Deep Heat in the underpants trick!

Stunts like that were commonplace and at one time you couldn't go into the dressing-room without having your clothes doctored in some shape or form. It would start off with knots tied in your trousers or your shirt and would progress to the toes of your socks being cut before things really started to get out of hand. Eventually clothes would go missing completely and of course Wally would be the prime suspect. Sometimes, even if he was completely innocent, players would wreak revenge by cutting the sleeves off his shirt. A red rag to a bull. Wally would then set about taking what started off as a light-hearted prank to the limit and on one occasion I remember him tearing one poor bloke's clothes completely to shreds.

I also remember the time when the apprentices were getting a bit cocky and every time we asked them to do something they would turn round and tell us where to get off. In order to teach them a lesson Wally went into their dressing-room one day armed with a dozen eggs and a bag of flour and proceeded to bombard the walls and the floor before leaving them to clean up the mess.

Yet for all Wally's tomfoolery he was a damned good player with a terrific footballing brain. He was a skilful player and he always used to claim he was above the Wimbledon long ball game, saying he could only play like his hero Rodney Marsh. The only thing that held him back was that he walked with a limp as a result of his cartilage operation. He could still play a bit but he didn't have the speed to go with his ability. He knew his stuff though and you would always listen to him if he had anything to say in the dressing-room because more often than not it made sense. It's just so strange that a bloke who could be so sensible one minute could be a complete lunatic the next. One thing for sure, though, life at Wimbledon wouldn't have been as much fun without Wally Downes.

One of his great rivals in the 'club looney' stakes was Steve Parsons, another great lad who epitomised the spirit of Wimbledon. My fondest memory of him is from a party I staged at a local hall to celebrate my 21st birthday. All the lads were there. The party was in full swing when someone said, 'Where's Steve?' We found him up in the attic sitting on a window ledge throwing potted plants in the air and cracking them on his head. The original crack pot you might say!

You need people like Steve and Wally around the place, just

94

as you need the straight men like Lawrie Sanchez – Mr Sensible – and the moody ones like Alan Cork – Mr Depressive as we called him. Lawrie, who didn't come to the club until the end of 1984, became my room-mate and my biggest pal at the club – despite the fact I took the captaincy from him a few years ago and then stole his glory in the FA Cup final. He still goes on about the fact that, as the scorer of our winning goal, he was all set to become a Wembley hero and be acclaimed all

Dave and his close Wimbledon friend Lawrie Sanchez share a magical moment.

over the world until I saved the penalty and hogged all the headlines. Instead of raving about his headed winner people ask 'Who scored Wimbledon's goal that beat Liverpool?', and I don't think he'll ever forgive me for it.

He's dead straight but he has the sort of dry sense of humour which appeals to me and I had a lot of fun with him. He was never keen to get involved in too many stupid pranks himself but he'd encourage others to make fools of themselves. Sanch is very intelligent (he's got more 'O' levels than most of us put together – and a degree too) and he was the one other players turned to for help or advice on anything, and probably still do. He was Mr Encyclopaedia who knew the answers to everything. It did take him a while to settle in and be accepted into 'the family' and at one time he was accused of not being 100 per cent behind the Wimbledon cause. Now though there are few people with more blue and yellow blood searing through their veins than Sanch.

Corky is another loyal subject having been at the club since they entered the League in 1977, but it was only in my last few years at Plough Lane that he really came out of his shell. He was always the quiet one who rarely got involved in the crazy antics the club had become renowned for, but suddenly he changed and went completely loopy. Before then he used to mope around complaining that his hair was falling out and he was going bald at 25, or he'd be forever moaning about his dodgy leg which had a metal plate in it. He was worried that he looked a lot older than he was and now people at Chelsea come up to me and say things like, 'I thought Corky was about 30 five years ago', yet he's only just turned 30 now.

I imagine it must have been difficult for certain players to come into the club during those crazy days and some found it hard to get accepted into the scene. But, for the most part, a new lad would come in and take over where the last man had left off. You only have to look at the way people like Sanch, Fash and Vinny – by no means original members of the Crazy Gang – came in and imposed their own personality on 'the family'. That's been the great thing about Wimbledon, the continuity.

Vinny, for example, came in and almost immediately was at the centre of everything that went on. Now he's gone to Leeds someone else will take over the mantle. But, like Wally Downes, Vinny won't be forgotten in a hurry and, as far as the people who really know him are concerned, he won't just be remembered for the problems he had or the trouble he used to get into. Most of the things he's done on the field – from his sending off on the Isle of Wight to the infamous ballroom dance with Paul Gascoigne – have all been well-documented but, he's not as black as he's been painted in certain sections of the media. Sure he gets carried away from time to time and is prone to moments of madness, but there's another side to his nature which people aren't so keen to talk about. He's hard, yes, but not the villain he's made out to be. Take it from me, Vinny is a decent fella with a heart of gold – he certainly doesn't go round with blood dripping from his mouth. If you saw him pushing people around in wheelchairs or reading nursery rhymes to my kids, you would soon realise there's another side to Vinny Jones. He'd go out of his way to help you and I've got a lot of time for the fella. It's just that he got a 'bad boy' reputation early on and now he's stuck with it, probably for the rest of his career.

A lot of it stems from the time when he made the break-through at Wimbledon and, for a start, revelled in the publicity he was getting – good or otherwise. But since getting that reputation people are just waiting for him to overstep the mark. If you focus a camera on Vinny for 90 minutes you'll find a morsel to make a meal out of, his punishment for a gesture he made to Mark Falco at QPR last season being a perfect example. Those sort of things go on all the time without warranting a mention in the Press but because it was Vinny it made headline news. He's served his time and now he deserves to be left alone to concentrate on his football, because he can play a bit too, you know. Maybe his move to Leeds will do him good and instead of being the 'leader of those Wimbledon hooligans' he can start afresh at Elland Road.

My earliest recollections of him go back to the time when he was on trial at Wimbledon and breezed into the place so noisy and confident that you felt he'd been there for years. I remember Wally turning to me at the time and saying:'He's a bit loud for a trialist, isn't he?' That was rich coming from Wally but I think he felt a bit put out because here was a cocky 'Jack the lad' steaming into his patch. In actual fact, in the short time they were at the club together, they got on great. They were both unpredictable and Vinny carried on the mantle when Wally left. It always makes me smile to recall how Vinny would carry a ghetto blaster around with him all the time and he even took it into the dressing-room with him when we went to Anfield for the first time. We won 2-1 and after the game his favourite 'house music' was blaring out as we danced around the changing-room. It later emerged that the sound could be heard all the way down the corridor and the Liverpool apprentices got a right rollicking from Ronnie Moran for dancing to the Wimbledon music. It was little things like that which made Vinny such a valuable figure to have around and he got on well with everyone.

It was with big Fash, though, that he struck up the greatest friendship and for the most part the pair of them were insepa-rable, both looking up to each other but for different reasons; Vinny to Fash because of his image and charisma, and Fash to Vinny because he enjoyed having a hard man like 'Psycho' alongside him. They would look out for each other off the field as well as on it. Fash, who had a lot of friends in boxing circles, used to be seen around with a man-mountain called BJ and we used to wind him up about having a minder. Shortly after we'd seen BJ get knocked out in a televised fight the mickey-taking got worse and Sanch would take Fash to task saying things like, 'Fancy having a minder with a glass jaw.' Fash took the bait and said: 'Flipping heck, Sanch, I wouldn't like to see you in the ring with him.' Sanch, with his dry drawl, insisted he'd be happy to take up the challenge saying: 'With a glass jaw like that I'd knock him out with one punch'. Maybe it was because of all this that Fash liked to go around with Vinny.

He's certainly very conscious of his image and when you've got as much going for you as Fash I don't blame him. I know he comes across as flash and arrogant but the bloke's done well for himself – he's even a TV presenter now – and most criticism levelled at him is borne purely out of jealousy. I wish I had been doing as well as him at 25. Come to think of it, I wouldn't mind being a quid behind him now! He's done everything . . . even had lunch with the Queen – not that something as trivial as that would cut any ice with the lads at Wimbledon. I'm sure they would have taken the wind out of his sails by suggesting that he was sitting no nearer the Queen than the geezer in the hot dog stall at the back of the room. The lads at Plough Lane know how to bring somebody back down to earth.

Like Vinny, who scored the winner against Manchester United in only his second game for the club, Fash also made an immediate impact on the field. He was bought for a club record fee towards the end of the 1985-86 season to help in our final push for promotion to Division One and he did exactly that with a number of vital goals on the run-in. From the first game he played for us I considered him to be everything you'd look for in a centre-forward and I remember thinking to myself at the time: 'Fash, you'll do for me, son.' Harry bought him to win promotion for us and he did it so inevitably he was an instant hit with the fans and, like Vinny, became something of a cult figure at Plough Lane overnight. In fact the two of them were rarely out of the headlines because of their high-profile images. In a way that used to annoy some of the other lads and I can understand it to a certain extent because they had played their part in the club's meteoric rise as much as anyone. I'm sure they still get fed up from time to time hearing 'Fash this' and 'Fash that', but you can't help but like the fella.

He doesn't mind people having a go about his image because he's got the sense of humour to carry it off. Sanch would always take the mickey out of some of his clothes but Fash would simply strike back by saying: 'Well, Sanch, if you've got a weekend to spare you can come and have a look round my wardrobe.' Fash has certainly got a way with words although he does have a humorous tendency to get certain catchphrases mixed up, like the time he converted Harry's phrase 'Charlie big potato' to 'big time Charlie jacket potato'.

At Wimbledon it doesn't matter who you are or what you earn, at the end of the day you are still just one of the lads. You can be everything and yet a nobody, or be a nobody and mean everything to the people around you. I've had people come up to me and say that Fash is getting too big for the club but my answer every time is: 'I'd sooner have Fash playing for me than against me.' As long as he's pulling his weight within the framework of the team, the lads don't care what he's doing off the field. If he ever stopped doing his stuff on the park then you might have a bit of bother, but I can't see that happening – not even now he's won his England cap. He'll be missed when he goes but like the rest of us he can be replaced and, as long as the team sticks together, Wimbledon can continue to hold their own in the top flight . . . and have a lot more fun along the way.

A lot of players have come and gone in recent years but things haven't changed a great deal and, while the current gang may not be as crazy as their predecessors, even under Bobby Gould there's time for a laugh and a joke. It's up to new players to conform to what's going on around them, not the other way around. The lads wouldn't go out of their way to make them feel welcome, they had to earn the right to be part of things. That usually means being the butt of a few jokes for a while. If you can take it you're all right. If you can't then Wimbledon isn't the place for you. But it's not just the ability to take a joke that makes a good Wimbledon player. As anyone who's played for the club will tell you the management work you bloody hard too.

In fact of the three clubs I've now played for training at Wimbledon was more physical, more intense than any of them. At Plough Lane we accepted that we weren't blessed with the talent some other clubs had so we had to make up for it with sheer hard work and team spirit. It's something the club has always thrived on and no doubt will continue to do so. That doesn't mean to say that there weren't arguments along the way; we had our rucks at Wimbledon just the same as any club. But they were soon forgotten about and weren't allowed to lead to anything which might have upset the smooth running of the club. Harry, for instance, could blow his top after games (I've lost count of the number of times he kicked over tables and chairs or threw cups around the dressing-room) and give you a right slagging off, but he'd always come up and have a drink with you in the bar afterwards. He never used to go away and sulk or bear a grudge.

He was the sort of bloke you could talk things out with and, if you had a grievance, he was always prepared to listen. The only problem was that you could go in and see Harry about a pay rise and, using his ability to talk the hind legs off a donkey, he would somehow manage to turn the issue round. He would say things like:'You should consider yourself lucky to get paid for doing something you enjoy, there are people out there far worse off than you, you know'. You would end up going along with everything he'd said and come out having virtually agreed to take a cut! In fairness to Harry he would have given us extra money if he could, but there wasn't the cash in the coffers for him to do that. At the end of the day he motivated you so much that you wanted to go out and play for him, not the money. That's the sort of influential character he was and I have nothing but admiration for him.

He was the one who gave me a start in the game (and he's never let me forget it either!) and I shall always look up to him, always listen to any advice he has to offer. But then I'm used to listening to Harry, especially to the medley of stories he would keep us amused with at one time. He would have me in stitches with some of the tales of his career (most of them totally unprintable) but the trouble with Harry was that he would then proceed to tell the same stories every time a new player arrived at the club. After the 20th time of hearing them, they weren't funny any more. Only joking, Harry! He was literally one of the lads and just because he was manager didn't mean he was exempt from the odd wind- up.

There was one occasion during an end-of-season break in Spain when, after a few glasses of the old falling down water, we raided his room while he was out. He came back to find virtually all the contents of his room – including his bed – floating in the hotel swimming pool. A similar thing happened the night before the final match of the 1986-87 season at Sheffield Wednesday, Harry's last game in charge of the club. Because there was little at stake he said that we could have a beer or some wine with our dinner and later he even let us go into town for a drink 'as long as you don't go mad'.

Before we left the hotel Harry, who'd been entertaining guests, walked up to reception and placed his key on the desk. Fatal. Sanch and I nicked it without him noticing and, while he was away, we went up to his room and wreaked havoc. We ran a bath and put his jeans in, tied all his ties up in knots, put talcum powder in his socks and underpants and finally stripped his bed before putting it in one of the lifts. When he eventually made his way back to his room he found his bed in the lift and calmly went down to reception and said: 'Find me another room – and charge it to the players.' The best thing was that he didn't think me and Sanch were capable of such a trick and he blamed Vinny. Even more amusing was the fact that, despite our unusual preparations for the game, we stuffed Wednesday 2-0 to send Harry off in style.

He managed to see the funny side of that one but there was another occasion in Spain when he was anything but amused by our late-night high jinks. It happened towards the end of a boozy evening when we were midway through a night club crawl and Harry left saying he was off to the next one. Former Wimbledon player Mick Smith and I didn't believe him so we decided to follow him and, sure enough, he'd taken the route straight back to the hotel. As he made his way round the last corner we decided to jump him but as we ran towards him he turned round like a startled rabbit with a terrified look on his face. We didn't know what to do next but, as there was a fountain outside the hotel, we thought 'what the hell' and threw him in, fully dressed. We were laughing our heads off but he just got up, climbed out of the water and stormed inside the hotel without saying a word. It wasn't like Harry to react like that and we really thought we would be in for a rollicking, so the next morning we went up and apologised for being out of order. He still looked annoyed but said:'Don't worry lads, I'm the one that should be sorry.' He was disappointed with himself for his reaction to what was just another Wimbledon prank and it turned out that he'd only got the hump because we'd ruined his new canvas shoes.

Physio Derek French was another of the so-called backroom boys who was game for a laugh. He also had a terrific singing voice and one night at Frank McLintock's pub near Kings Cross – after we'd won the Fourth Division Championship – he completely upstaged the live band Frank had paid for with his version of *High-heeled Sneakers*. He went down a storm. The players provided the backing vocals and we must have looked a rare old sight with knotted bar towels on our heads and snooker cue chalk on the end of our noses. Good job nobody knew who we were. We certainly couldn't have got away with that sort of thing after the Cup final, for example, because it would have made front page news. Frenchy and Harry were brilliant together and it was no surprise when he followed the gaffer to Watford. I was disappointed to see them go but, certainly as far as Harry was concerned, he felt he'd done all he could for Wimbledon by that time.

To me Harry wasn't just a manager I had the utmost respect for, he was a close friend too. An indication that he holds me in the same high regard came when he invited me and just one or two of the old guard from Wimbledon to his 40th birthday party. I considered that a great privilege and a tremendous gesture on his part. It was also a great party! Someone had arranged for a scantily clad kiss-o-gram girl to come along and do her bit, but true to form Harry managed to upstage her by dropping his trousers as she read his birthday poem. By the time she'd finished he had even fewer clothes on than her. It was typical of Harry – and it didn't cost him £750 either!

That was how much each of the players were fined for a similar act of 'indecency' after our FA Cup final triumph when we hit the headlines for our infamous 'moonie' at Plough Lane. It was all done as a joke at Corky's testimonial and we certainly never intended to offend anybody. We just didn't expect our backsides to be splashed all over the papers, although the FA clearly thought it was premeditated and designed to make us a few extra quid. In actual fact it was a spur of the moment thing prompted by cries from the Wimbledon fans of 'Vinny, Vinny show us yer bum'. Vinny duly obliged and one or two of us followed suit but it wasn't until half-time that we decided to provide the fans with a team photo with a difference. It was all a bit of harmless fun and we never thought for a minute that it would land us in such trouble with the soccer authorities. It cost us £750 each – and even more when we had our appeal turned down. We had to smile, though, when the *Daily Mirror* used the picture for a spot the ball competition, carrying with it a caption which read something like: 'For all you readers with dirty minds, it's under so and so's foot!' A few days later they ran another competition using the same photo, only this time you had to identify the players from their backsides. Standing between two midgets in Dennis Wise and Terry Phelan I was instantly recognisable because my bum was about a foot higher than theirs. It was my last outrageous stunt with the Crazy Gang – and probably the most infamous – before my move to Newcastle and, although we were hauled up before the FA, it was an appropriate way in which to sign off. Bottoms up, lads!

Skipper Dave Beasant (front row, far left) basks in the glory of his and Wimbledon's greatest day.

The greatest moment of his career – Dave proudly raises the FA Cup aloft after the dramatic Wembley victory over Liverpool.

*The happiest man in town. Dave in jubilant mood with the coveted
FA Cup.*

Two views of Dave's sensational penalty save from John Aldridge which made him the first 'keeper to stop a spot-kick in an FA Cup final at Wembley.

Proud father Dick Beasant is the happiest dad in town as he shares a special moment with Dave and grandson Nicky.

CHAPTER SEVEN

The End of an Era

The celebration champagne which flowed long after our Wembley triumph had scarcely had time to go flat when managing director Sam Hamman dropped a bombshell. Within days of the final he told the Press that every Wimbledon player was up for sale – at the right price. I must admit that it seemed a strange thing to say after we had just won the Cup and the club was, presumably, looking to build on that success. When you see that sort of thing in the papers it makes you wonder about the ambitions of the club and it was as though he was saying: 'We've won the Cup and that's as far as we're going to go.' Having already toyed with the idea of leaving Wimbledon myself his remarks made me think that slapping in a transfer request wouldn't be a bad idea. I'd done well in the Cup final in front of a massive, worldwide audience and now seemed as good a time as any to make the break. The fact I had only one more year of my contract to run made it all the more likely that, if the club WAS going to sell me, they'd do it now rather than later. Out of contract Wimbledon couldn't expect to receive anything like the fee they could get with our Wembley wonder show still fresh in the memory.

But my eventual departure from Wimbledon had nothing to

do with any disagreement with Sam. Nor did my transfer to Newcastle have anything to do with his refusal to pay the players any bonus money for winning the FA Cup – although that was one of the few things which disappointed me about my last days at Wimbledon. It all came about in the week leading up to the final when, as captain, I was arguing on behalf of the team that our bonus agreement, which had been signed long before we'd ever looked like reaching Wembley, should be revamped in the light of our fantastic Cup run. We had got money for each round up to the final but there was no reward for actually winning it. All we were entitled to was our appearance money, which seemed crazy. We got extra money for winning League games but not the FA Cup. It wasn't that we were looking for any extra incentive to beat Liverpool – knowing the FA Cup was there for the taking was incentive enough – but it was a matter of principle. The financial rewards the club received for us getting Wimbledon to Wembley (from gate receipts, TV rights, etc.) were phenomenal but the players wouldn't see any of it. I argued with Sam that we deserved this and we deserved that but all he would say was: 'You signed the bonus agreement so you should stick by it.'

In actual fact bonus payments for the FA Cup, which didn't include the final, were agreed two or three years before when Wembley was just a ground I used to pass on my way to work. Suddenly I was going there to play my part in the game's greatest showpiece and getting nothing for it. I got knocked back by Sam so many times it was untrue and every time I relayed the bad news to the lads the atmosphere at the club became more and more intense. There we were, preparing for the biggest game of our lives and the club had a revolt on their hands. It all seemed so unreal.

The situation almost reached crisis point when we travelled back from our last League game of the season at Old Trafford just five days before the final. The players were sitting at the back of the coach having a discussion (we called our get-togethers 'crisis meetings' and this literally was) and we came up with a plan designed to put pressure on the club to alter their stance. We were aware that, for the Cup final itself, the club was planning to change the sponsors' name on the front of our shirts from 'Truman' to 'Carlsberg'. Both belonged to the same company – Truman being a subsidiary of Carlsberg – but they wanted a different name on the shirts to exploit the mass coverage the sponsors were going to get. It may not sound an important issue but it was to the club and the sponsors – and we knew it. That's why it was suggested we should refuse to wear the new shirts out of protest. We threatened to tell Sid the kit man to bring the old 'Truman' shirts along to Wembley and we would slip into them on the big day. The more we discussed the matter on that infamous coach journey back from Manchester the more rebellious the players became, to the point that at one stage someone chipped in: 'I know, let's not play at all.' We decided that a complete boycott of the final wasn't the answer but the fact that someone even suggested it gives an indication of the strength of feeling in the camp at the time.

It was, of course a silly idea because no one in their right mind would give up the opportunity to play in a Wembley Cup final. I certainly had no intention of doing so and suddenly I had to assume the role of 'Captain Sensible' in order to put things back into perspective. The truth is that the lads would have walked out at Wembley with Mickey Mouse on their shirts if it meant playing in the game's great showpiece. These were all idle threats borne out of frustration and disappointment.

The repercussions of an incident which happened a few weeks before the semi-final were also being felt at the time and they simply added to the unrest among the players. They still remembered how, after the dressing-rooms at our training ground had been broken into, the club refused to allow us to make claims on Wimbledon's insurance for the things we'd had stolen. Watches, jewellery and a bit of cash went missing and, because a lot of the gear had belonged to young lads still living at home with their parents, they weren't covered on household insurance. I had a watch stolen and wasn't covered either but it was the young lads I felt sorry for and I fully expected the club to help them out. They refused, saying that, as the training ground wasn't owned by Wimbledon FC, the club wasn't liable for any losses incurred. Technically they may have been correct but what had happened to the compassion and the friendliness on which the club had been built? I went in to see Sam but he wasn't prepared to set a precedent which might have more far-reaching repercussions in the future. I was annoyed that the dressing-rooms weren't safe in the first instance but even more furious with the club's reaction.

I brought the matter up again during my discussions with Sam over bonuses. It was clear I was bashing my head against a brick wall so, as a last resort, I suggested to him that if we went on to win the Cup it might be a nice gesture on the club's part to buy the lads a new watch with something inscribed on it as a 'thank you'. He said he'd think about it and, for all I knew, he probably did give it some thought. But he never did anything about it – not until I'd gone to Newcastle anyway! I discovered some time later that the lads who played in the Charity Shield match against Liverpool got their bonus money after all while myself and Andy Thorn, who also joined Newcastle, got nothing. So all my wranglings with Sam paid off in the long run but I wasn't around to reap the benefits. I felt a little hard done by and thought that, even though I'd left, the club could have paid me too. After all, I did play my part in putting the FA Cup in the Plough Lane trophy cabinet. I didn't have a chance to follow up the matter before I received a phone call from the secretary at Wimbledon asking me what I'd had stolen from the dressing rooms months before. He claimed that he'd only just discovered we hadn't been compensated. I found it difficult to believe considering that it had been in all the papers (I was quoted several times) but they insisted something would be done about it.

As captain at the time I had done most of the talking, to Sam and the Press, and it must have looked as though I was having a go at the club I was about to leave. One newspaper article bearing my name carried the headline 'Wimbledon: you meanies' and it portrayed both me and the club in a bad light. I never wanted to cause trouble though, I was just trying to make sure that the players got what they deserved. I might have spoken out about the unhappy state of affairs at the time and maybe some of my comments made Sam out to be the bad guy. But there was no ill-feeling between us when I left. In fact we still get on great and even now he accepts me back into Plough Lane with a smile, a customary tug of my curly hair and a few friendly words in his native Lebanese. At least I assume they're friendly!

After the final there had been a few rumours, mainly linking me with Tottenham, but as far as I was concerned it was nothing more than paper talk. At that stage I was happy to savour the victory over Liverpool and bask in the glory of being the FA Cup winning captain. I certainly never considered the final to have been my last game for Wimbledon. It wasn't until I spoke to Gouldy a couple of weeks afterwards that I realised there was more to the speculation than met the eye. I asked him if he had heard anything and he said, 'No, why? Have you been tapped up?' I assured him I hadn't and he asked if I would consider going to Newcastle if they came in for me. They had made an offer earlier in the year but nothing had materialised. He had turned them down originally, because of the Cup run, but this time I could sense he was seriously considering letting me go. I told him that I would certainly agree to meet them and having been put on the spot by Bob I said I would probably sign for them given the chance and the right deal.

He explained that they had been showing interest again and he was expecting them to come back with an offer for me. But that was all he said. I asked him how much he would want for me and I couldn't tell whether he was joking or not when he said: 'After what you did in the final I'd want a million for you.' A few days later, a Saturday morning, he phoned me at home about nine-thirty in the morning and said that Newcastle had put in a bid and Wimbeldon had agreed a fee so it was down to me. He said he didn't want me to go but he wouldn't stop me talking to them. I asked him again what the fee was but still he wouldn't tell me. Shortly afterwards I received another phone call, this time from Willie McFaul explaining that he had made an offer which Wimbledon had accepted and he asked me if

I would go and talk to him. I had nothing to lose so agreed to meet him at a hotel on the M1 midway between London and Newcastle. He didn't want me to fly up to Newcastle in case I was spotted at the airport or going to the ground. He wanted to keep it hush-hush so we had a secret rendezvous.

I left myself two-and-a-half hours to reach my Derby destination but I should have known London traffic better than that and it took me well over an hour-and-a-half just to get to the other side of Luton. Once on the open road I drove like a bat out of hell and even if any police had seen me it's unlikely they would have been able to catch me. I was supposed to meet Willie at two p.m. but there was no way I was going to make it and I began to worry that I would miss him and lose out on the dream move I'd always craved. Thankfully Willie was caught up in traffic too and, as luck would have it, we both arrived at Normanton Hotel at the same time.

At the time Gazza, Paul Goddard, Peter Jackson and Neil McDonald were all still at the club and he told me he had the makings of a good side. He explained that Gazza was likely to be on his way but hoped everyone else would be staying and that the future looked good. He outlined to me what he felt the club was capable of achieving and said that he saw me as the missing link. What he said impressed me and I liked him as a fella too. After the talks I didn't commit myself there and then, preferring to go home, talk it over with the wife and sleep on it for a while. I didn't want to jump straight in and say 'Give me the pen, where do I sign?' because there were a lot of things to think about – both sides of the touchline. Bearing in mind that this was the beginning of June and that we'd only won the FA Cup a few weeks before, it was all happening very quickly. As a result of my performance in the final I was very much in the news and, with the talk of other clubs being interested, Willie obviously wanted to get in first. He was keen to get me to sign before the stories hit the papers and other clubs became aware and turned the thing into an auction.

As it happened I spoke to Willie on the Saturday and before I'd put pen to paper the following Thursday, it was in the Press that I was going to sign for Newcastle. West Ham and Spurs were both interested but I don't think they were prepared to match the £850,000 fee Newcastle had come up with.

I must admit that, at the time, I was half hoping that Spurs would come in with a bid because a move across London to White Hart Lane would have been ideal for me. Tottenham is a big club and I remember thinking at the time that if I could pick any team in the country to play for, it would be Spurs. I would have loved the opportunity to talk to them. They are my home town club and a move there would have been everything you look for as a player. Unfortunately, while I understand Spurs did make a bid, their player plus cash offer didn't suit Wimbledon. They wanted the money. In any case I don't think Bobby Gould would have wanted me to go to another London club, so the move was never meant to be. I couldn't have gone much further away than Newcastle.

As it turned out Spurs ended up paying a small fortune for Gazza, leaving Newcastle with enough money to spend on me to frighten off any other would-be buyers. So really, at the end of the day, my choice was simple; join Newcastle or stay where you are. When the day of reckoning came I was flown up to Newcastle to sign and it was a day I will never forget. I received the sort of treatment I thought was only reserved for super-stars, not lanky goalkeepers. When we arrived at the airport in Newcastle we were met by a posse of photographers, reporters and TV crews. It was as though I had just got off the plane with The Beatles. Everyone, it seemed, from the stewardesses to the luggage handlers, was patting me on the back and wishing me luck. The welcome I got was unbelievable . . . and I hadn't even signed for them at that stage. I had been in the public eye after the Cup final but this was something completely new to me because it was on such a large scale. I dare say it took a few people by surprise, it even shook me how quickly the whole thing happened. One minute I was a Wimbledon hero at Wembley, the next I was talking to Newcastle and on the brink of leaving the team I'd played for all those years.

I'm sure the Wimbledon fans were taken aback by it all but they had been given a warning by Sam's statement to the Press suggesting that we were 'all' available at the right price. We were all in the shop window at Wembley and because we had done so well the valuation of each player had shot up and Sam wanted to take advantage of it. For example, Newcastle's bid in January was £350,000 and Gouldy told them to come back with a decent offer which he felt should have been in the region of £750,000. At the time I thought he was pricing me out of the market and that no one would want me at that figure. After all Chris Woods was the most expensive keeper at £650,000 and Gouldy was putting me at £100,000 more than that. I remember thinking that for a team to pay that much it would make me Britain's most expensive goalkeeper and I just couldn't see that happening. As it turned out, the figure Newcastle were prepared to fork out was £200,000 more than the record. Crazy. It was good business for Wimbledon though and a move was something I had wanted for a while so I was delighted too.

When Newcastle made their original bid in January I had discussed the pros and cons of such a move with Sandra and we both agreed at the time that if something was sorted out between the two clubs we would be prepared to go to Tyneside. That's why when they came in a second time it didn't take us too long to think about it. We had already crossed that bridge only to be sent back. Now we were going over the river again. As it turned out I was glad Bob didn't let me go in the first instance because I would have missed out on the Cup run. But then again, if I had left Wimbledon, the club may not have got to Wembley anyway or even won the Cup. You just never know. Perhaps the time wasn't right then and fate was lending a helping hand. I remember Bob saying after the FA Cup triumph: 'I bet you're glad I didn't sell you straightaway.' As it turned out he had done me a great favour, but when Newcastle came in again after the Cup final, then it was right to go and even the Wimbledon fans came up to me and said I was making the right decision. I think they were surprised because it was so soon after the Wembley triumph but I think they understood and a lot of them were very good about it. They even thanked me for what I had done for the club and I received a lot of mail wishing me well. One letter in particular summed up the situation perfectly. It said: 'You have been good for Wimbledon and we're sorry to see you go but the time is right for you to move on.' I don't think the fans were suggesting I had outgrown the club – I certainly didn't feel that way – but what they did accept was that I done as much for the club as I possibly could.

I wanted to go to a big club and after giving Wimbledon good service for so long it was my chance to be overpaid for once. I'd been looking over the garden fence at next door's swimming pool for too long; now it was my turn to sample life on the other side. I earned a decent living at Wimbledon but there comes a time when you want to join a more glamorous outfit and be pampered a little bit. Wimbledon is a great club and one I will always have a lot of affection for, but it is also a very small club. The players and the management are First Division standard, there's no doubt about that, but the set-up in terms of the ground, the support and the finances leave a lot to be desired. The stadium and its offices are still Fourth Division standard. That's why it was such an incredible achievement for us to win the FA Cup. But Liverpool knew they would be back at Wembley the next time, and they'll probably be there the year after too, while the Dons might never make it to the final again. That's the difference between the two teams. Short of winning the Championship how can Wimbledon improve on that success? I couldn't see them doing that in my time. They'll also continue to play in front of small crowds at Plough Lane and I wanted to savour the big-match atmosphere week in, week out. So there were lots of things which influenced my decision to leave.

Money was another factor and while it wasn't the be all and end all of everything, it was important to get the right deal – not just for me, but my family – at that stage of my career. I was 29 and everything had to be right. I want to look after my wife and kids the best I can, no one can blame me for that. The deal Newcastle were offering was so much better than I could have dreamed of earning at Wimbledon. Everyone used to moan about us being underpaid and the board would simply counter our complaints by explaining that, because of the size of the club and the paltry gates we were attracting they couldn't afford to pay the players as much as we perhaps deserved. My feeling all along was that it wasn't the players' fault that the club was only getting average home gates of around 7,500. We were doing our bit on the field, finishing sixth in the League and winning the Cup. That's the difference between Wimbledon and Newcastle. Even when Newcastle are struggling they are guaranteed home gates of around 20,000 – that's because the football club means more to the people on Tyneside than Wimbledon means to people in South West London.

The move also presented me with the opportunity to press for an England call-up. Wimbledon players rarely get international recognition and I honestly believe that there are players at Plough Lane, or at least there were, who would be regulars for their country if they were with a different team. I couldn't see that changing. At the age of 29 I wanted a taste of the high life and the glamour that goes with playing for a big club. And they don't come much bigger than Newcastle. I remember going to St James' Park with Wimbledon in the FA Cup the year we went on to win the trophy and they had just opened the new stand. It looked so impressive and I remember wondering what it must be like to play for a real First Division club. The set-up was superb, they owned their own training ground and it was everything I imagined a big club with a lot of tradition to be like. It was the type of place I had always wanted to be associated with and that's one of the reasons why I was so happy to join them. After years of 'slumming' it, if you like, I was up there with the big boys. It was the realisation of a dream I had harboured for years and years and even though it meant giving up my testimonial at Wimbledon it was well worth it. I could have hung on at Plough Lane for the remaining year of my contract, collected a few bob from the testimonial and then said my farewells. At that time I would have been a free agent and, as the transfer fee would not have been so high, the clubs that couldn't afford the £850,000 Newcastle coughed up might have come in for me and I would have had more of a choice.

You get a gut feeling when the time is right to leave, and this was it. I didn't think it was worth taking a chance on getting a big move in a year's time because anything could have happened in the interim. I might have had a bad year, picked up some serious injuries. You just don't know. It wasn't an easy decision, though, and it did seem strange to be leaving Wimbledon after so many years there as a player. I'd been through everything with them and it wasn't so much leaving a club as turning your back on a family. That's how close we all were at Plough Lane.

It all came home to me during the summer when, after I'd committed my allegiance to Newcastle, I went along to the Wimbledon tennis championships with all my old team-mates. It was an invitation the Cup final squad had received after the Wembley triumph and was the tennis club's way of paying tribute to the football club. Even though I'd officially left Wimbledon I didn't want to miss out on the day, but it did seem strange being together with the lads knowing that I wouldn't be leading them into battle any more. It was as if I was still a Wimbledon player, and I remember experiencing similar emotions when I went to Wembley to watch them play in the Charity Shield against Liverpool a week before I made my League debut for Newcastle. Sitting in the stands waiting for the kick-off I felt more nervous than I had done as a Wimbledon player before the final. I was concerned for my young successor Simon Tracey, my understudy for four years at Plough Lane, and I was desperate for him to have a good game. And, although the lads lost 2-1, Simon did really well and I was delighted for him. It was a weird experience watching him in action in the yellow shirt I'd made my trademark as a Wimbledon player – he even went through the same warm-up exercises as me. It was like watching a cardboard cut-out of me with a different head on.

I have to confess that I felt very envious of the lads being out on the hallowed turf again and couldn't help thinking that I should have been out there with them. After all, I'd done my bit in booking Wimbledon a second Wembley visit. After the match the lads came up to me with their losers' medals in the hands saying: 'You haven't got one of these, have you Dave?' We also had a joke about some of the cutting comments Alan

Cork had made about me in the Press on the morning of the game. In the build-up to the match I'd been interviewed by one of the national papers and was quoted as saying that Bobby Gould was mad to leave Vinny Jones out of the team because of his controversial sending off in a friendly on the Isle of Wight. What I'd actually said was that, such was the code of conduct at Wimbledon, it was probably right for Vinny to be left out but that the lads would miss him. The upshot of it all was that I received a phone call from Bob saying he was reporting me to the FA over the comments I'd made. He claimed I was out of order telling him how to pick his team and basically he was telling me that I should keep my nose out of his affairs.

That was also the essence of a counter story Alan Cork had printed in the *Daily Mirror* in which he was quoted as saying that players who had left the club should mind their own business and keep their mouths shut. He also suggested that Thorny and I were greedy and had only gone to Newcastle for the money, saying sarcastically: 'Well, they haven't gone for the scenery have they?' His comments really annoyed me and were right out of order because if there was one player at Wimbledon who used to moan about money and continually go on about getting away from the club it was Corky. Even the other Wimbledon lads felt he had spoken out of turn against a so-called mate. I'm not averse to speaking my mind but I would never have a go at individuals like that, especially someone I'd known for so long, and when I saw him after the game he looked all sheepish and whispered to me: 'I only did it because the paper was paying me for it. The more I said, the more I got.' I just turned round and said to him, 'If you want to sell your soul to the papers, Corky, that's up to you.' Apart from that there's been no real animosity between me and the club – and it's not true that Bobby Gould and I fell out over what was really a storm in a teacup. We are still on speaking terms. In fact I saw Bob after the Charity Shield and he was as nice as pie when he spoke to me. The funny thing was that before he went on his way he turned round and said: 'Oh, by the way, you do know I've reported you to the FA.' Thanks, Bob.

It was disappointing that my long and happy association with Wimbledon should end on something of a sour note, but it wasn't as if I was slagging off the club. How could I do that after all the happy years I'd spent there? I would never do that because you never know when you might come to need those people again. I might even end up back at Wimbledon in a coaching capacity. Time's a great healer and I'd like to think I'll be welcomed back to Plough Lane for years to come.

CHAPTER EIGHT

A Different World

With a new season and a new era beckoning, the series of niggly events which closed the book on my Wimbledon story were soon forgotten. At least they were on my part. I was too busy concentrating on my new career in a soccer-mad city where only 100 per cent commitment and allegiance to Newcastle United is considered good enough. All I'd achieved and enjoyed at Wimbledon was history; I was a Newcastle player now.

Ironically, though, it was with my old club in mind that I set about my first task on Tyneside – playing my part in the signing of former Plough Lane team-mate Andy Thorn. It wasn't a case of trying to put one over on Wimbledon; more a case of giving Andy a glowing recommendation to Willie McFaul. I was away on a pre-season tour of Sweden when Andy put pen to paper for Newcastle (like me for £850,000), but I'd known about the club's interest in him for some time. I was aware that Thorny was a bit unsettled at Wimbledon – after what Sam Hammam said in the papers I dare say everyone was – and that, despite being named captain, he was keen to fly the nest. Something had obviously gone on between him, Bob and Sam with the result that Thorny had asked for a transfer. Knowing that he was unhappy at Plough Lane, I suggested to Willie that he could be the answer to the defensive dilemma which was facing Newcastle. At that time Glenn Roeder hadn't returned to the club for pre-season training, having gone south in search of a player-manager's job, and we needed a centre-half. Willie said he was looking for a player with experience and, while Thorny was still only a youngster, I assured the boss he had an old head on his young shoulders. In my book he was the man for the job, a player with terrific potential.

Willie asked me how much he might cost and I explained that, as Andy had signed a two-and-a-half year contract just before the Cup final, Newcastle had better get a cheque ready for £500,000. That was the last I heard until we were away on tour when Thorny joined us for £850,000. I was a bit surprised at the size of the fee because he'd only been in the first team at Wimbledon for two years but it was another example of how the club's success had inflated players' values. When the news reached us in Sweden some of the lads came up to me and said that one of my old team-mates would be joining us. Bearing in mind that Willie had told me not to mention anything about Andy's transfer through fear of unsettling the defenders already at the club I had to play 'Mr Naive' and ask politely: 'Really, who's that then?' They then started to ask me all about him and I told them exactly what I'd told Willie a few weeks before; he was a good, solid player who would do a great job for us. I don't think I convinced everyone of Andy's worth and I could sense that his big money transfer, following hot on the heels of mine, annoyed a few of the players – especially the home-grown lads who resented the fact that outsiders were coming in and possibly earning more than them. I could see in their attitude and their expressions they felt hard done by.

In addition to me and Thorny, John Robertson and John Hendrie had also arrived at the club during the close-season for big fees and all the talk before the big kick-off was of the new lads and what a difference we would make. The lads who'd been at Newcastle for some time felt they were in danger of being overlooked by the boss when the new team

All smiles at the Newcastle photo-call as Willie shows off his new signings last summer. Dave is flanked by Andy Thorn with John Hendrie (left) and John Robertson bringing up the rear.

took shape. I was disappointed with the attitude of some lads and my view was that they should either stop whingeing or find another club where they wouldn't feel harshly treated. If you complained about every new player that came into the club, the team wouldn't get anywhere. As for their concern about the money they were earning, again the solution was simple – ask for a transfer to a club where they would be guaranteed the cash they felt they deserved. As a newcomer myself I tried not to get too involved in the politics of it all, choosing to keep my thoughts to myself. But, coming from a club where camaraderie was a key word and where everyone looked out for everyone else, it was a strange introduction.

The fact that the fans were hailing me as something of a saviour probably went against the grain with a few people too. When I first joined Newcastle, supporters would come up to me in the street and say that the one thing the team at Newcastle had always lacked since Willie McFaul's day was a good goalkeeper. It was nice that they thought so much of me but by lifting me up and placing me on a pedestal they were putting a lot of weight on my shoulders. It was then I realised exactly how much was expected of me. In their eyes I was second to Jesus – and I was probably expected to perform miracles too. The magnitiude of the club, and the task I'd undertaken, became clearer as the start of the season drew closer.

I also received something of an insight into the club from the coach at the time, John Pickering, who, on our arrival in Newcastle, invited Sandra and myself round to his house for dinner. He made us feel immediately welcome and it was good to get to know a member of the Newcastle staff before I started training with them. We had a good chat and I appreciated him taking the time to put me in the picture about what would be expected of me at a club where the fans demanded success. He also gave me an idea of what I could anticipate in terms of training. I was trying to feather my own bed by saying that, having been in the game for ten years, I was used to certain training methods and I was too long in the tooth to change them. Whether my words cut any ice with John I don't know but he warned me not to expect any favours just because he'd invited me round for a meal. Before I left he told me not to tell any of the other lads I'd been there and he said his goodbyes by concluding: 'I might have been nice to you tonight, but when you see me on the training ground don't expect me to be so kind.' What he was trying to tell me was that, while we might be friends away from the training pitch, on it we must have a working relationship.

The next morning I made my way to the training ground to meet my new team-mates and was immediately impressed with the facilities. The lads helped me settle in quickly and made me feel welcome by introducing themselves in turn. The one person I was a bit wary of meeting, however, was Mirandinha whom Thorny and I had both clashed with when Wimbledon beat Newcastle in the FA Cup a few months previously. When I joined Newcastle I was keen to play the incident down, explaining to the local Press that it was all forgotten about and there was no ill-feeling on my part. I still wasn't sure how Mira would react, however, but I needn't have worried because as I was getting changed for training the door opened and in he walked, shouting, 'Hello, big Dave . . . my friend', in his unmistakable accent. It immediately broke the ice and I can now see that what he did during the FA Cup tie was completely out of character. He's a smashing guy and that's what I told Thorny when he joined us. He had more reason to despise Mira than me after what happened but I assured him he wasn't such a bad guy and there was no point in trying to settle the score.

Off the field I settled in fairly quickly and didn't feel the sudden culture shock that everyone predicted I would encounter. I must admit I was surprised I adjusted so quickly myself because I thought it would take time to get London out of my system. I'd got a preconceived idea about the north being all coal mines and flat caps but when you get up there it's nothing like that. Newcastle is a beautiful place, far better than I imagined, and that was the only shock for me. A nice one, mind. The way of life is so much slower than London and the football more important to the people than you find in the capital. At Newcastle hundreds turn up just to watch you train! You are always in the public eye and it keeps you on your toes.

Playing six matches in Sweden before the start of the season provided me with the ideal opportunity to really get to know my new team-mates. Mind you, I must admit I wasn't exactly relishing the prospect of a boat trip from Newcastle across to Scandinavia – all 26 hours of it! Thankfully it was quite a smooth crossing and the fact we were allowed a few drinks in the bar before sleeping through most of the journey meant it wasn't the drag I feared. Shame the same couldn't be said of the return voyage. Having had a few drinks after our last game I wasn't feeling all that clever by the time we climbed aboard the ferry bound for Newcastle at six o'clock the next morning. If I was looking a bit pale at that point I was positively green by the time we got back. I must have looked as though I had got a 'keeper's jersey pulled over my head. The old North Sea gave the boat some stick and I was bad all the way home. When you're out there in the middle of the ocean there's just no escape from it and I felt like death by the time we pulled into Newcastle. The lads were suitably sympathetic, of course. I vowed there and then that if we ever went back to Sweden I would fly there – even if it meant paying my own way.

I was still feeling a bit rough when we played Dundee in a friendly a few days later. We lost that game 2-0, a result and display which brought us back down to earth after we'd won every match in Sweden – and played some lovely stuff too – albeit against second-rate opposition. Unlike the Swedes, Dundee never allowed us a second on the ball and instead of us playing the ball out from the back, as we had done abroad, I was having to kick the ball long every time. Without a big man up front we were getting nowhere. It was a problem we hadn't encountered in Sweden and it served as a warning of what could lie ahead for us. It hit us like an electric shock and sent panic waves around the squad as we wondered how good we really were.

A few days later we played non-League Whitby Town and tanked them 5-1 which was all very nice but they hardly provided us with the sort of opposition we were going to come up against in the First Division. The game was more for Whitby's benefit than ours and even though we won convincingly the game could have done us more harm than good because it rebuilt the false sense of security that was in evidence when we came back from Sweden. The next match, away at Peterborough, promised to provide us with a tougher test but we ran out comfortable 7-0 winners, with Mirandinha getting four in the second half. Again it was a good win but there was no point in getting carried away and I couldn't help asking myself, 'Are we that good, or is the opposition that bad?'

The Newcastle Press were full of praise but the Dundee result was still preying on my mind and causing me concern. My early doubts seemed to be justified in our next friendly at Second Division Blackburn when we went in at half-time 2-1 down. But our lacklustre first-half performance was the last thing on my mind when Willie pulled me to one side at the interval, pushed me into the showers and told me that he'd had a message from the police explaining that my youngest son Sam had been rushed into hospital. All sorts of horrible thoughts were rushing through my head and it transpired that Sam had fallen out of a chair, banged his head and been taken in for X-rays. Willie pulled me out of the action and I rushed off to hospital fearing the worst and expecting to find Sandra in tears. Thankfully it wasn't as bad as she first thought and the X-rays revealed that there was no damage to the skull which was a relief to us all.

Nobody in the Press knew about the drama and the papers the next day were full of stories to the effect that I'd dropped a clanger in the build-up to one of Blackburn's goals and was hauled off by the boss at half-time as a result. It wasn't until later that the real story came out accompanied by such sensational headlines as 'Beasant in hospital dash' prompting the national papers to pick up on it and blow the whole thing out of proportion. Apart from all that I had very few problems settling in on Tyneside or adjusting to a new way of life. The only problems I was to encounter were on the field – as I soon found out.

Before my first League game for Newcastle, away at Everton,

I'd heard that six or seven thousand Geordie fans would be making the trip to Merseyside (that's as many as we used to get at Wimbledon for a home game!) so I was expecting quite a reception. But the greeting we got was way above anything I'd anticipated, or ever received before. Even as early as two o'clock – an hour before the kick off – there were about 4,000 Newcastle fans inside the ground and I couldn't believe the noise they made when we walked out to inspect the pitch. The chanting was incredible and something I'll never forget as long as I live. So you can imagine what the atmosphere was like when we went out just before the kick-off with the stadium packed to capacity.

It was turning into a day full of surprises for me because earlier that morning I'd received the biggest shock of all . . . Willie McFaul made me captain. The boss broke the news during the pre-match chat and I couldn't believe my ears. There had been no indication I would be skipper as, during pre-season games, Peter Jackson and Dave McCreery had shared the job in the absence of regular captain Glenn Roeder. I honestly thought one of them would get the job and you could have knocked me down with a feather when the boss handed me the skipper's arm band. Willie said that, as I'd been such a responsible skipper at Wimbledon, I was the man for the job. Who was I to argue? A few of the lads were messing about, winding me up about my appointment, and I dare say some of them must have thought, 'why has he got the job, he's only been here five minutes?' There was no animosity or jealousy though and I was a very proud man indeed – especially when I heard the fans chanting my name before the start of the match. I kept putting my hand to my ear pretending I couldn't hear them and each time their singing got even louder. We had an instant rapport. With myself, Andy Thorn, John Robertson and John Hendrie making our League debuts and Tony Cottee, Pat Nevin, Stuart McCall and the ex-Newcastle full-back Neil McDonald starting a League game in an Everton shirt for the first time the scene was perfectly set for a new chapter in the Dave Beasant story.

CHAPTER NINE

Tyne and Weary: A Newcastle Diary

Saturday, 27 August 1988   Everton 4, Newcastle 0

My head might have been in the clouds as we kicked off but it took just 34 seconds for me to be brought back down to earth – not so much with a bump as an almighty thud. Although my first touch of the game was to pull off a good save from Graeme Sharp, my second was to fish the ball out of the net after Tony Cottee had put away the rebound. What a start. We began to play a bit of football after that but within half an hour we were 2-0 down – and virtually out. Again it was Cottee who was doing his best to spoil my big day, this time with a tame-looking shot into the far corner. If I was honest I would have to say I was slow to react. Our lads were totally shell-shocked and, without wishing to blow my own trumpet, we would have been buried without trace but for a couple of saves I made late in the first half.

The second period was a similar story, Everton were just playing around us and we seemed powerless to resist. They got a third on the hour (Cottee again, needless to say) and Sharp wrapped it up with another after 84 minutes. We surrendered, simple as that, and didn't seem to want to battle and get back

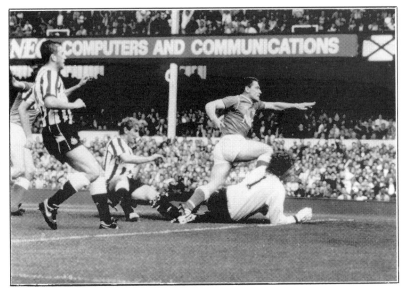

Just 34 seconds are on the clock and Dave has conceded his first League goal as a Newcastle player. Everton's Tony Cottee is the destroyer.

into the game. We have a lot to learn. From a personal point of view I did OK (even though I did let in four) and Cottee said afterwards that, had it not been for me, Everton would have won by nine or ten.

Monday, 29 August 1988   Newcastle 1, Wimbledon 0

Two games into the season and who should we draw in the Mercantile Credit Trophy? None other than my old club Wimbledon. The competition wasn't that important, but the Press had built the game up into something of a grudge match because Thorny and I were ex-Dons. Corky didn't need a second invitation to have a go at us and, having already had a pop in the papers labelling us 'greedy' he now reckoned he was 'sharpening up his elbows ready for war'. He also told the *Mirror*: 'I might be a lot older than Andy, but I've battled against tougher players than him. I'll show him who's boss.' As it turned out Corky wasn't even in the team, left out because he had a sore throat, would you believe? Must have been all that talking he'd done to the Press! One of my old team-mates it WAS good to see again was Lawrie Sanchez who, like me, was skipper on the night. Sanch and his wife were going out with me and Sandra for a Chinese meal after the game and, as I'd booked a table for ten past ten, I joked with the ref about making sure there was a result so we avoided extra-time.

No such luck. After 90 minutes the score was 0-0 and with another half-an-hour to play our meal was looking decidedly dodgy. There were only ten minutes left when Michael O'Neill smashed in the goal which meant Thorny and I could at least hold our heads up in the players' lounge afterwards. I had a drink and a chat with my old mates and I enjoyed meeting up with them all again. I enjoyed beating them even more. Oh, by the way, we were a little late arriving at the Chinese restaurant but got our meal after all.

Saturday, 3 September 1988   Newcastle 2, Tottenham 2

The return of Paul Gascoigne and, as you would expect, all the talk before the game was not of the match itself but of Gazza and the reception he would get. Apparently all the shops sold out of Mars Bars and most of them ended up on the St James' Park pitch. I thought it was all good-natured stuff until I discovered later that some of them were frozen solid. The players also had a frosty reception in store for the former Newcastle favourite and Willie McFaul was geeing us up beforehand saying, 'Get out there and show him what you can do', a reference to Gazza's verbal swipe about the club lacking ambition.

Not surprisingly, he and Chris Waddle were booed every time they touched the ball, but after just five minutes we had the fans cheering when Andy Thorn scored his first goal for the club. I was delighted for him because he'd had a rough ride so far and was trying too hard to impress. When Darren Jackson put us further ahead after 19 minutes we were cruising and the feeling amongst the lads in the dressing-room at half-time was that we had won the match already. Willie and myself tried to impress on everyone that we still had a lot to do but the warning didn't seem to do any good because, within a minute of the restart, Waddle pulled one back. The goal put the frighteners on us and our heads went down. They got a second after 64 minutes, but not before a controversial incident involving a few idiot fans. Waddle went over to take a corner and was bombarded by Mars Bars. A piece of brick was also thrown and, as he walked away, police were called in to restore order. Those fans didn't do us any favours because the hold-up caused us to lose concentration and Fenwick scored straight from the corner. What the manager and I feared might happen, did happen and Willie was right to have a go at us after the match. The thing I can't understand is the way that, after the slightest setback, we seem to crumble. We did it after their first goal and it's something we must put right.

Saturday, 10 September 1988   Derby 2, Newcastle 0

The Press had been building this game up for a while because when I joined Newcastle I made my international ambitions known and, as we were playing Derby, the match was billed as a Beasant v Shilton confrontation. Fair enough, I suppose, but the 'I want your shirt' headlines were a bit over the top. I hadn't said anything of the sort. But suddenly the pressure was on me to perform.

Before I could do anything about it we were involved in a real-life drama normally reserved for soap operas. For a start we had to have a police escort from the hotel to the Baseball Ground but the driver didn't have a clue about getting around Derby and when we finally reached the ground it was two-fifteen, the time the boss and I should have been presenting the team sheet to the ref. We were in danger of incurring a club fine for being late and, to make matters worse, we weren't allowed inside the stadium because there'd been a bomb scare. After a while Willie and I managed to persuade the police to let us in to see the ref and the lads followed later. But that wasn't the end of it. Before we got changed the police wanted all our gear checked to make sure the dressing-room was safe and we jokingly pointed accusing fingers at the Irish lads, Dave McCreery and Michael O'Neill, suggesting the police carry out a body search. All entertaining stuff you might think but hardly the ideal preparation for such an important match.

The kick-off was delayed to allow all the fans in and for the first 45 minutes of the match I think everyone's mind must have been on the bomb hoax because nothing really happened. After 66 minutes, however, Trevor Hebberd ran 20 yards with the ball completely unchallenged before firing in a shot from 25 yards. The ball flew into the top corner and didn't give me a chance, one of those shots which would have beaten anybody . . . even the fella at the other end. Suddenly we had our backs to the wall and, to be honest, we never looked like getting back in the game. I can't remember us having a shot at goal. With ten minutes to go Paul Goddard stole in at the near post to clinch the match and, as happened against Spurs, the heads dropped. That would never have happened at Wimbledon, but there's not the same spirit here and when things are going against us the players don't want to know. It's a mess but it can only get better, can't it?

Saturday, 17 September 1988   Newcastle 0, Norwich 2

Another bad result and I have to take a certain amount of responsibility for the first goal. Dale Gordon had a clear run at me and, from the angle he was running in at, seemed to be shaping for a cross. I tried to leave it but ended up helping the ball into the net. From then on we were in trouble. For their second goal a long ball forward put Robert Fleck clean through and as I came out to shut him down he lofted the ball over me and into the net. To complete my misery I caught him on the way through and was booked for a dangerous challenge although it certainly wasn't intentional. Although Norwich are currently top of the League and do play some nice football we had enough chances to beat them.

Wednesday, 21 September 1988   Manchester United 2, Newcastle 0

A break in the League programme and a visit to Old Trafford for the semi-final of the Mercantile Credit Trophy – and Mirandinha was back after injury to give the front line a boost. He didn't play from the start but when he came on with about ten minutes of normal time remaining and the score standing at 0-0 he must have had at least five cracks at goal. To say Mira likes to shoot on sight is an understatement; he'll have a dig from anywhere. But, as they say, if you don't buy a ticket you can't win the raffle so even though most of his efforts were off target at least he was having a go.

We went into extra-time confident of pulling off a result, but within a minute of the restart Steve Bruce put United 1-0 up. So, having gone a goal down, guess what happened next? We crumbled, of course. To look at some of our lads, losing a goal is like the end of the world and the heads drop as soon as the ball hits the net. It was no real surprise when Brian McClair got a second ten minutes later. Once that first goal went in there was no way we were ever going to get back into the match and, in fairness, we were lucky to lose by just two goals.

Saturday, 24 September 1988   Charlton 2, Newcastle 2

The pressure on Willie had been mounting and a lot of people claimed he wouldn't last the month, so we needed a good performance for his sake as much as the team's. Although we started badly we managed to hang on for 44 minutes, only to concede a sloppy goal just before the interval. Paul Stephenson was the guilty part this time, giving a stupid ball away on the edge of the box when he could have played a simple pass back to me.

When we went in a goal down at half-time Willie went potty and gave us a right rollicking. I think it did us some good because instead of heads going down it served to inspire us and, when Paul Miller was sent off for spitting at Darren Jackson, we were well on top. Darren took his revenge by equalising after 72 minutes and Brian Tinnion put us ahead soon after. It was time to kill the game but, with about three minutes left, we failed to clear a ball from our own box and Robert Lee mis-hit a half-volley which swerved past me and into the top corner. We didn't need telling we'd thrown it away (again) but, by the same token we didn't get the rub of the green either. We haven't had a League win all season and the pressure is beginning to tell.

Tuesday, 27 September 1988   Sheffield United 3, Newcastle 0

The second round of the Littlewoods Cup and, having already played my ex-Wimbledon team-mates in the Mercantile, I'm suddenly face-to-face with my old boss Dave Bassett, the new manager at Bramall Lane. United were sitting pretty at the top of the Third Division, having scored 22 goals in their first six matches, while we were near the bottom of the First, having scored 17 goals less! The ingredients were perfect for an upset but we were confident our First Division class would tell.

It didn't. Willie had asked me and Thorny what to expect from a Bassett side and we warned the lads of the threat of an aerial bombardment. We obviously didn't take heed because within five minutes we were a goal down. Half an hour later it was two and suddenly WE looked like the Third Division side. In the second half we played much better but they got a third goal to leave us with a mountain to climb in the return leg.

Afterwards Willie was lost for words which was probably a good thing because I'm sure he would have torn a few heads off. John Pickering wasn't so controlled, however. He lost his rag completely and started hurling pots of tea and cups around the dressing-room in his fury. Some players had boiling hot tea running down their legs but were too frightened to scream or say anything in case Pick jumped down their throats. He was lucky he didn't hurt someone badly but, when things had cooled down, we joked about having half-a-dozen players on the treatment table tomorrow with third degree burns. Pick told us that we could cost Willie his job and we knew we'd let him down. That performance was spineless and beyond a joke. While we didn't need to abandon our First Division principles, some of our players have got to learn that there's a time and place for the long ball. I'm not saying we should play the Wimbledon way, but perhaps we could do worse than take heed of a saying we had at Plough Lane which went something like: 'The opposition can't score when the ball's in Row F.'

Saturday, 1 October 1988   Liverpool 1, Newcastle 2

I'd said to some of the lads a couple of weeks before that we probably wouldn't win a League game until we came to Anfield, so now I'm considering quitting the game and becoming a clairvoyant. The win couldn't have come at a better time for Willie who was celebrating his 45th birthday and might have been receiving more cards than he bargained for. Defeat would have been the final nail in his coffin, of that I'm certain. The local Press were slaughtering him and we needed three points for his sake.

We started off slowly, as usual, and contrived to concede a goal to Gary Gillespie after just three minutes. I thought to myself, 'Here we go again, this is going to be a real trouncing.' But to my surprise, after I'd pulled off a few good saves (one from my old Wembley adversary John Aldridge) we started to get into it and John Hendrie scored with a breakaway goal on the half hour. In the second half we were really under the cosh but we defended well. In fact our back four were throwing themselves into so many challenges with such passion that, at one point, we had three men down injured. The commitment which had been missing all season was suddenly there for all to see and we got our reward when we were awarded a penalty with about seven minutes to go. Substitute John Robertson, who was on the sidelines waiting to come on at the time of the incident, was our usual penalty taker and he came racing on the pitch to take the kick. But, remembering how Zico missed a spot-kick after coming on the field in the World Cup, I screamed at Robbo to leave it. He was still cold so Mira took the responsibility and calmly struck the winner. What a captain!

At the end the Newcastle fans went mad and Willie came on the field to shake everyone's hand. We threw him in the bath with his clothes on, but I don't think he minded. To some of the lads this was like winning the Cup, but it just goes to show that, when we apply ourselves correctly, we can compete with the best. For the first time this season we defended as a team so maybe this result can be the turning point. Happy birthday, boss.

Saturday, 8 October 1988   Newcastle 0, Coventry 3

In recent weeks the crowd have been getting restless and chants of 'sack the board' are becoming commonplace but, after the win against Liverpool, we were expecting a big gate. We got over 20,000 for the visit of Coventry and the fans gave us a hero's welcome.

Within minutes of the kick-off, however, the same old cries were ringing around St James' and by half-time they were going wild. We were 3-0 down by that stage and the atmosphere inside the ground was hostile to say the least. I had never known anything like it. People were scrambling over seats and bodies to get to the directors' box to hurl abuse at the board, and various sections of the crowd were even fighting amongst themselves. It was ludicrous. I could understand their frustration to a certain extent, though, because for much of the game we didn't look as if we were going to get a kick. They turned right against us, so much so that they were cheering when Coventry got the ball and booing when we were in possession. Although we didn't concede any more goals in the second half the fans were still up in arms and hundreds of them congregated outside the main entrance to the ground. Their anger wasn't aimed at the players or the manager, however, it was the board they really had it in for. They want the current directors out and the consortium headed by John Hall – The Magpie Group – in. I don't understand the ins and outs of the situation but I do know that something has got to give . . . and soon.

As it turned out it was Willie who had to pay the price for our disastrous start. After beating Liverpool last week we were all of the opinion that we had turned the corner, Willie's job was safe and we could set about the task of climbing the table. But seven days later we were suddenly back to square one and, by Monday, were minus a manager. It just goes to show what a fickle business we are in because little more than a week before, Willie was being hailed a great boss, now he's been made the scapegoat when really it is the players who are to blame. Colin Suggett has been put in charge, for the time being at least, but it wouldn't surprise me if he doesn't last that long.

Wednesday, 12 October 1988   Newcastle 2, Sheffield United 0

A good win but we're still out of the Littlewoods Cup. Various players, myself included, had gone on record in the Press as saying that we would 'win for Willie' and although we didn't get the 3-0 victory we wanted we acquitted ourselves very well on the night. It's just a shame we didn't show more of that commitment and determination when Willie was in charge. Perhaps we'd have saved him from the chop.

The way we started the game we really looked as though we could get the three goals back but we had to wait until the 43rd minute for our first goal, courtesy of John Hendrie. The feeling in the dressing-room at half-time was that we could still do it and when Mira scored within a minute of the restart a remarkable comeback was on the cards. United looked as though they had cracked and Robbo had a great chance to equalise, but Dave Bassett has clearly instilled some of the famous Wimbledon spirit into the Sheffield ranks and they managed to hang on for a 3-2 aggregate win.

Although we were out of the competition, the 14,000 fans who turned up applauded us off the field. Mind you, they did start chanting sack the board again straight afterwards which

A lonely man. Former Newcastle boss Willie McFaul had no one to turn to in his hour of need.

140

just goes to show that booting Willie out achieved nothing in their eyes. They want the board out, full stop.

Saturday, 22 October 1988   West Ham 2, Newcastle 0

Having spent the early part of the week with the England squad preparing for the World Cup qualifier with Sweden I didn't train with the Newcastle lads and only met up with them on Friday night. When I did there seemed to be an air of confidence about the camp that's been missing most of the season. I hoped that would be a good sign but, even playing against the bottom club West Ham (they were one point behind us before the game) we couldn't raise our game.

We started the game reasonably well and were denied an early goal by the woodwork. Five minutes before half-time we suffered even more bad luck when Thorny got a kick in the head and needed lengthy treatment before he could get back to his feet. When the game restarted West Ham had a corner and Thorny asked me who he was supposed to be marking. I told him he should pick up Alvin Martin and he replied: 'Which one's he?' I asked him if he was alright and he said 'Yes' but when he faced the wrong way for the corner I knew he was in trouble. I had to physically turn him around and direct him towards the ball and it was no surprise that he didn't make the second half. Funny thing was that he thought we were 3-0 up at the interval. Maybe the physio should have knocked a few more out!

Ten minutes into the second half Alan Dickens stuck one past me but, for a change, we didn't bottle it and we stuck to the task. Late in the game their young forward Stuart Slater came racing through and I rushed out of my box to clear but only succeeded in flattening the poor sod. There were 'send him off' chants ringing around the ground and they started again when I brought the same player down inside the box late in the game. Ray Stewart scored from the spot. There was more drama to come when Paul Ince broke Michael O'Neill's nose (accidentally by all accounts) to cap a miserable afternoon.

One player in hospital with concussion, another with a broken nose and a 2-0 defeat to boot – what more could go wrong? Plenty, as it turned out, because the lads missed their train home to Newcastle. I stayed in London.

Wednesday, 26 October 1988   Newcastle 3, Middlesboro' 0

An all-ticket local derby meant there was a real buzz about the place before kick-off. In fact the atmosphere was electric and, with so much local pride at stake, there was an eagerness and a will to win in the players' eyes I had seen all too rarely. As skipper it was good to see everyone so fired up but I couldn't help thinking, 'Why aren't they like this all the time?' We hit the post early on and I wondered if it was going to be one of those games, but after half-an-hour we got the break we needed when Gary Pallister headed into his own net following a free-kick. The goal set the place alight and gave the players confidence to produce the kind of football I always felt we were capable of. In the second half Mira really got the bit between his teeth and was taking everyone on. He got his reward with two goals and we cruised to a 3-0 win. Suddenly the fans were right behind us and Tyneside is a great place to be at the moment.

Saturday, 29 October 1988   Newcastle 0, Nottingham Forest 1

Going into the game we were full of confidence and optimistic we could put our poor start behind us once and for all. There was a spirit about the side which had previously been missing . . . and it showed in our performance. We completely dominated the match and Forest didn't get much of a look in. In fact I hardly had a save to make and that's what made defeat to a Lee Chapman goal so difficult to accept. We didn't deserve to lose. Even the goal was a fluke. It came after 64 minutes when

Chettle put in a cross from the right and the ball hit the heel of Chapman and rolled inside the near post when the Forest striker had been aiming for the far corner. It was a sickening blow and one we didn't recover from, so you can imagine how low we all felt in the dressing-room afterwards. It was typical of the sort of luck we have been having this season. One of these days we are going to really hammer someone. One day.

Saturday, 5 November 1988   QPR 3, Newcastle 0

With QPR's plastic pitch now a thing of the past the lads were pleased to be playing on grass . . . until we saw the latest Loftus Road offering, that is. We couldn't believe the state of the surface, especially down one side of the field where it looked as though they had been holding tractor races. And the goal area was a nightmare for a 'keeper, mainly bare and hard with tufts of grass here and there. It was a disgrace. I spoke to England colleague David Seaman before the game and he warned me to be on my guard and watch the bounce very carefully. What a sport.

As for the game itself, we bore no resemblance at all to the team which hammered Middlesbrough the other week. Maybe we allowed ourselves to be beaten by the pitch. Rangers went ahead after only 12 minutes when Brian Tinnion headed a Trevor Francis cross on to our bar and Danny Maddix followed up to score on the rebound. The second goal was even more annoying because both Michael O'Neill and Darren Jackson were at fault, not once but twice. First of all they allowed Maddix to nick the ball from them and then stood and looked at each other as he waltzed through to set up Martin Allen for Rangers' second. It was a good strike by Allen, but a stupid goal to give away. There was plenty of endeavour on our part but no end product and, in the 83rd minute Falco made it 3-0.

I can't believe we can dominate a game in that manner and still lose by three goals so I had a bit of a moan in the dressing-room afterwards saying something like, 'It's no good having all the possession if you can't put the bloody ball in the net.' I think I upset a few players but they couldn't argue with the fact that we let QPR off the hook today. Despite the arguments the atmosphere among the players is still OK and, while everyone hated me at the time, they soon came round to my way of thinking over a drink in the bar.

Saturday, 12 November 1988   Newcastle 0, Arsenal 1

Arsenal are without doubt the team in form at the moment and most of the talk in the papers before the game was of how many goals they would get against the bottom club. We were determined not to be the whipping boys and we did quite well on the day although once again we never really looked like scoring. In the second half Mira was clean through and should have scored but allowed Lukic to make a save. We looked good value for a draw though, until Paul Merson came on for Rocastle and completely transformed the game. He forced me to make one good save and from the corner Bould scored with a looping header which went over me and into the far corner. But the most annoying thing about today's performance was the way we bottled it once their goal went in. Not for the first time this season, the heads went down and we stopped running and working. It was nothing short of criminal and some people are going to have to adopt a different attitude if we are to get out of trouble.

Saturday, 19 November 1988   Millwall 4, Newcastle 0

Before the game our fans were all talking about how much they were looking forward to going down to Millwall – whether it was the game or a possible confrontation with the Lions' notorious supporters they were relishing, I don't know. They certainly wouldn't have got any enjoyment out of our performance because, basically, we were hammered. Not even the presence of two new signings, Rob McDonald from

PSV Eindhoven and Liam O'Brien from Manchester United, inspired us. We were awful. Having had three midgets up front most of the season – 'The Subbuteo Men', as Mira, John Henrie and John Robertson had been tagged – we were hoping that big Rob McDonald, all six-feet-four-inches of him, would provide the aerial threat we had been lacking. But it wasn't to be. Millwall went ahead after 26 minutes when Alan Mcleary hit an unstoppable volley past me from 20 yards and a minute before half-time Terry Hurlock killed us off with a shot from the edge of the box which deflected off John Anderson and went through my legs as I dived. We didn't really have an answer to Millwall's long ball tactics and on the hour Tony Cascarino made it 3-0 with a near post shot I should have saved. At 2-0 down we were still battling but as soon as they scored the third we threw the towel in. It was no real surprise when we went 4-0 down because we didn't have an answer to the no-nonsense style of Millwall whose commitment was reminiscent of my old club Wimbledon. It may not look too pretty but, combined with their impressive work-rate, it's a damn sight more effective than the way we are playing at the moment.

The defeat came on a day when stories in the Press were linking me with Spurs (amongst others) and, as I didn't travel back to Newcastle with the lads, I'm sure Colin Suggett thought I was staying behind in London to have talks with Terry Venables. To add even more fuel to the fire I was involved in a verbal ruck with Suggy and his assistant Mick Martin before the team left to catch their train home. After a result like that I couldn't believe that nothing much was said in the dressing-room and I felt a few things should be aired while we were all together. If Wimbledon had just lost 4-0 under Dave Bassett my old boss would have been f'in and blindin' and throwing cups of tea around the dressing-room in disgust, but Suggy just isn't like that. He's too mild-mannered for a manager and was happy to say nothing. I wasn't, and after I started the ball rolling Mick Martin turned round to mè and said something like:'You let a goal in through your legs and you've got the nerve to have a go at the rest of the team.' It started getting petty and I hit back saying:'I'm sorry Mick, but I'm not too good on deflections so you'd better start looking for a 'keeper who is.' With all the Spurs talk in the papers earlier you can imagine what everyone was thinking and I must admit, for the first time since joining Newcastle, I was really down in the dumps and asking myself: 'What the hell am I doing here?' To go from the England bench in Saudi Arabia in midweek to this, all in the space of a few days, was soul-destroying and all sorts of thoughts were racing through my mind as I made my way home. Mick was out of order to have a go at me like that and right now I'm not a happy man.

Sunday, 27 November 1988   Newcastle 0, Manchester United 0

By the time this live TV game had come around I had settled my differences with the management. In fact I had clear-the-air talks with Suggy two days after the Millwall game when he asked me if I was happy at the club. He was convinced I was looking to get away but, having had time to think about the situation, I assured him that Newcastle was the only club I wanted to play for. We also spoke about where the team was going wrong and he pointed an accusing finger at the back four. I agreed that our defending left a lot to be desired but added: 'How can you expect the defence to improve when we never practice that aspect of our play in training?' At Wimbledon we always practiced our defensive techniques twice a week and, by the time the game had come around on the Saturday, players were doing things out of habit. That's not been the case at Newcastle and the crazy thing was that it needed me to point this out.

For the first time this season we set to work on our defensive techniques and it paid handsome dividends against United. The game may not have been a classic but we came out of it with some credit and, for a spell, United were there for the taking. Having said that, our opponents did have the ball in the net on one occasion, but Brian McClair was seen by millions to charge me over the goal-line with the ball in my grasp. In the end we were happy to settle for a draw.

One player who wasn't too happy, however, was Mira who came in for some stick from a section of the fans today for what they considered to be a selfish performance. No one minds when his runs into no-man's-land come off and he scores

Dave in action during his brief spell with Newcastle. Despite the ups and downs he was happy on Tyneside.

spectacular goals from crazy angles and distances but when he screws up the fans are on his back faster than you can say Mirandinha. And they really seem to be turning against him at the moment. The trouble with Mira is that the last thing on his mind when he gets the ball is to lay it off. 'Pass' is not one of the English words he's picked up yet and his sole aim is to go for goal which is fine when things are running for you but frustrating for everyone else when we are struggling. He did waste a fair bit of possession today and a few harsh words were said to Mira by some of the other lads in the dressing-room afterwards. He can understand most of the points we are trying to make but when tempers are frayed and voices are raised, as they were today, he struggles to grasp what's going on. When we are all ranting and raving it must sound Japanese to him and there are times when I feel sorry for him. Today he must have felt that everyone was against him because all our dressing-room discussion (for want of a better word) seemed to involve him and it was 'Mira this, Mira that, Mira the other'. I'm not one to row with him but there was one occasion today when I had to bawl him out because he came deep to collect the ball and was trying to do his tricks in front of our own box which is not on. I told him in no uncertain terms where to perform his heroics so he probably thinks I've got it in for him as well.

Saturday, 3 December 1988   Luton 0, Newcastle 0

There's nothing like a good, exciting game of football and this was nothing like a good, exciting game of football. 'The yawn of the season' I think one publication called it and the reporter wasn't far wrong. Mind you, we were happy with a point on plastic, even happier not to have conceded a goal for the second week running. Our passing, particularly early on, was very sloppy and we were our own worst enemies at times as we insisted on trying to play the ball square across the back four. Suicide. We had a couple of let offs in the first half, but could have won it in the second when Liam O'Brien had a goal disallowed for offside. On the whole, though, it was a dull game with little atmosphere inside the ground. The few hundred Newcastle fans who made the journey down made more noise than the Luton supporters and I think they must have been happy to go home with a point. It seems we finally have our defending sorted out, now all we need to conquer is our goal-scoring problem. Nine goals from 15 League games (none in the last six) is pitiful and we don't look as though we are ever going to win another game.

After the match we travelled up to Manchester for the Guinness Soccer Sixes starting on Sunday and, on the way up, there was a news flash on the radio saying that Newcastle had made an approach for QPR boss Jim Smith. The lads had known nothing about it and, judging by the look on Suggy's face, he was none the wiser either. There hadn't been anything in the papers, no speculation, nothing. It came right out of the blue. Colin came up to the senior lads on the coach and asked them to keep mum about the news. If anyone asked us about it we were told to say nothing. It must have come as a real shock to Suggy and I think we all felt for him. You would have thought that the club would have had the decency to tell him that they had approached Jim Smith rather than letting him discover the news via the media.

Saturday, 10 December 1988   Newcastle 2, Wimbledon 1

Sure enough Jim Smith was named as Suggy's successor and what a start we made under the Bald Eagle – a 2-1 win against my old Wimbledon mates. You could sense that everyone wanted to do well for the new manager but that sort of attitude never ceases to amaze me. Why didn't they try that hard when Willie or Suggy was in charge? Still, the new boss does seem to have breathed new life into the club and hopefully this can be the start of a new era.

We hadn't scored for six games before today so it was quite a relief when John Hendrie put us ahead after 41 minutes following good work by new boy Kevin Brock. Knowing how Wimbledon play, Thorny and I were able to give the other lads a few pointers, such as the threat from Vinny's long throws, Dennis Wise's corners and Hans Segers' long kicks. Mind you, Vinny caught me out with one of his throws in the second half when I misjudged the flight of the ball and couldn't recover in time to stop Terry Gibson scoring with an overhead kick. Vinny had put one over on me and I was bitterly disappointed with myself.

Overall though, I enjoyed coming up against my old mates again, and had to smile at some of the remarks aimed at me. Every time I kicked the ball long and it came straight back, one of the Wimbledon lads (normally Vinny) would say: 'Hey, Dave, they are not as good at that as we were, are they?' There's nothing wrong with a bit of banter between mates and it was all taken in good part with no animosity involved. In fact there didn't seem to be the same do-or-die attitude about Wimbledon generally today. Maybe they were holding back because they felt sorry for me and Thorny. To cap an eventful day Hendrie popped up to score the winner with ten minutes left so at least I was able to hold my head up in the bar afterwards.

Tuesday, 13 December 1988   Watford 2, Newcastle 2

The third round of the much-maligned Simod Cup and although we kicked off with what I considered to be our strongest side it took just six minutes for fate to deal us yet another blow when John Anderson went off with a pulled hamstring. Despite the set-back we started well but, as has been the case all too often this season, we failed to convert possession into goals. We went a goal down after 50 minutes when the offside tactic backfired on us and, although Rob McDonald equalised soon after, we were out of the cup when Paul Wilkinson scored a late winner after good work by my ex-Wimbledon and Newcastle team-mate Glyn Hodges. Things didn't work out for Glyn on Tyneside but, after coming on as a 75th minute sub, he showed our travelling fans what he was capable of with a jinking run, a nutmeg and a spinning cross which Wilkinson tucked away.

After tonight's performance I think the boss realises he's got to strengthen his squad – a new striker being his top priority. There have already been a few stories in the press linking him with John Fashanu and I, for one, would be delighted to see my old mate in a black and white striped shirt.

Saturday, 17 December 1988 Newcastle 3, Southampton 3

The boss has begun to wield the axe by selling Darren Jackson to Dundee United and John Robertson back to Hearts, and he's made it clear that everyone is playing for his place. Even me, I shouldn't wonder.

Kevin Brock, signed from Jim Smith's old club QPR, served notice of his intentions by scoring a brilliant opener after just seven minutes but, within 20 minutes, we were 2-1 down and struggling. The three Wallace brothers were causing us all sorts of trouble with their pace and Glenn Roeder, for all his skill and knowledge of the game, was left wanting for speed as the terrible trio ran riot. Matthew Le Tisser got their first two goals and Rod Wallace seemed to have put the game beyond our reach with a third after 54 minutes. But, with half-an-hour left, the boss made an inspired substitution by replacing Mira with Michael O'Neill and the young Irishman scored with virtually his first touch. With a minute to go Michael struck the equaliser and almost completed a remarkable hat-trick with seconds left when he hit the bar.

Not surprisingly, Jim Smith was raving about Michael after the game but he shouldn't let this performance mask the fact that we are lacking pace at the back. We conceded three goals today because of bad marking and lapses in concentration and, in our present predicament, that's something we can't afford to happen. But to come from 3-1 down and get a point shows there's more character about the side than there was earlier in the season, so that's something to be grateful for.

Monday, 26 December 1988   Sheffield Wednesday 1, Newcastle 2

Full-backs Ray Ranson and Kenny Sansom joined the club before Christmas to add some experience to the side and both were in for their debuts today. They are two good signings and Kenny in particular is going to be determined to get his career going again after languishing in the reserves at Arsenal and he'll do a good job (as skipper, as it later turned out!).

We made the worst possible start today and I think the lads at the back must have still been running their turkey and Christmas pud off when David Hirst scored after three minutes. To our credit, though, we didn't buckle and eight minutes later Rob McDonald struck the equaliser. Just before half-time Michael O'Neill, in from the start in place of Mira, scored one of the jammiest goals of the season. He looked as though he was going down in the area for a penalty when the ball hit his shin and went in. He claimed he was always in control but I have my doubts. The important thing was that the goal gave us three valuable points. We had to hang on a bit at the end, especially as Thorny was hobbling around up front with ankle ligament trouble, but it was a good result and we deserved the win. The only disappointment was the injury to Thorny and the fact that he's going to be in plaster for a month. We got the victory we wanted, but at a price.

Saturday, 31 December 1988 Tottenham 2, Newcastle 0

With confidence high after three games without defeat we started well and played some good football for the first 20 minutes . . . too much football as it turned out. In trying to be too neat, too clever, we allowed ourselves to be hit on the break twice in the space of ten minutes and suddenly we were

2-0 down, Walsh and Waddle the scorers. In the second half it was all Spurs and I had to pull off a few saves to keep us in the game. But when Mira came on for the last 20 minutes he could have had four goals, and would have but for the brilliance of Bobby Mimms who surprised a few people with his display at a time when he was supposed to be struggling.

All in all we had NINE good chances so it was little wonder Jim Smith blew a fuse in the dressing-room afterwards. There's obviously something wrong when you don't convert any of them and the boss must be worried about that aspect of our play. Terry Venables looks to be building a useful side which will be challenging for the title next season and I have to admit that it crossed my mind more than once today that I might have been a Spurs player.

Monday, 2 January 1989   Newcastle 0, Derby 1

As seems to be the case every match day on Tyneside the wind was blowing at something just short of gale force – and as usual we were blowing hot and cold. Although we played well in the first half we couldn't find a way past Peter Shilton who was confounding his critics with another immaculate display of goalkeeping. One stop he made from John Hendrie was world-class and he was at his best to pull off a superb double save from Michael O'Neill and then Kevin Brock. Who said he's over the hill?

But while Shilts was in fine form, the boss had a go at us at half-time for showing my England colleague too much respect and being frightened of his reputation. He was annoyed that players weren't prepared to try their luck against him and were 'passing the buck' instead of shooting themselves. Fair comment, I thought, because Shilts was certainly winning a massive psychological battle out there today.

In the second half we paid for our lack of adventure when Mark Wright headed home from a free-kick to give Derby the points they didn't really deserve. But that's what you get when you fail to take your chances and I wasn't too surprised to hear the crowd turn against us. They started booing certain players and singled out Rob McDonald who, from being the hero in recent weeks, was suddenly the villain for missing a number of chances. After he missed one volley the fans booed him every time he touched the ball and sarcastically cheered when he hit another shot over the bar. It just goes to show how fickle the supporters can be. I can understand their frustration but the players need them behind us, not on our backs.

Things are not going too well for me at the moment, especially at home where the odd error seems to be creeping into my game. Away from home I've been playing well, making great saves and looking in command, but at St James' Park I have not performed so well and the fans are not seeing the best of me. There are still transfer speculation stories about me in the papers but Jim Smith has said nothing to make me think he's going to sell me to buy the outfield players he needs.

Saturday, 7 January 1989   Newcastle 0, Watford 0

I remember how, when Jim was named manager, he wasted no time in pulling me to one side and asking me if I was happy at the club and then saying he was concerned about a 'keeper being captain, despite the fact he made Dave Seaman skipper at QPR. He hinted that it wouldn't be long before he would make an outfield player captain and, as soon as he signed Kenny Sansom, I knew my days as skipper were numbered. He didn't do it straightaway but when it finally happened – yesterday afternoon, to be exact – I was bitterly disappointed, although I could understand the boss's reasons. Having said that though, I believe I did a good job for Wimbledon and likewise for Newcastle as a goalkeeping captain and felt I had the respect of the players. But, if that's his choice, who am I to argue? When he asked me how I felt all I could think to say way: 'It's up to you, it's your decision.' I was hurt all right but I wasn't going to let him see that.

I didn't speak to Kenny about it until just before today's FA Cup third round tie with Watford and when I walked into the treatment room just as Jim was giving him the captain's arm band, he seemed a bit embarrassed by it all. He admitted he was surprised to be named skipper so soon, but there was no animosity involved on my part. It was an honour to be captain and while I'm not happy about relinquishing the job it won't affect the way I play.

As for the game, it certainly wasn't a classic and a 0-0 draw was probably about the right result. After all the memorable moments of last season's FA Cup competition this was a bit of an anti-climax but at least we're still in with a shout . . . just.

Tuesday, 10 January 1989   Watford 2, Newcastle 2

Having driven down to London with the family on Sunday I didn't see the lads until I arrived at the team hotel last night. When I walked into the lobby I was surprised to see Jim Smith engaged in conversation with Chelsea boss Bobby Campbell. I knew Jim was looking for a striker and my immediate thought was: 'Oh great, we're going to sign Kerry Dixon or Gordon Durie.' I never imagined for a minute that they would be discussing my future. In fact I thought no more of it and the incident was the furthest thing from my mind when we kicked off the replay.

The game, however, began disastrously for me because in the first minute I was alleged to have handled outside the area when kicking the ball away. I'm convinced I didn't commit an offence but the ref gave a free kick and Neil Redfearn scored from the edge of the box. Fortunately Brocky equalised after leaving Paul Miller on his backside just before the break and we went in at half-time on level terms. Once in the dressing-room I protested my innocence over the free kick which led to the goal and I was stunned to learn from Jim Smith that the Watford management team had been into the referee's room before the game to tell the linesmen to keep a close eye on me when I was kicking the ball out. Frankly, I was disgusted and it seemed to me that the linesman who pulled me up had been influenced by what he'd heard before the kick-off and got carried away. The incident didn't seem to matter when Mirandinha, who had missed a couple of chances in the first half put us 2-1 up from the penalty spot five minutes after the interval. In fact I even allowed myself a moment to daydream about a possible return to Wembley. I should have known better because after 63 minutes we were on level terms again when the referee went hand ball-crazy, awarding Watford a penalty when Ray Ranson had the ball blasted against him. It was a diabolical decision and I could do nothing about Redfearn's kick. The game went into extra-time but, with no more goals scored, we've got to do it all again next Monday.

After the game I stayed behind to have a chat with some old Wimbledon mates, Vinny Jones, Nigel Winterburn and Mark Morris, who had been watching the game from the stands. I was enjoying the reunion until I spotted Newcastle reporter Alan Oliver with a face as long as a wet weekend in Brighton. He looked so disappointed and I said to him: 'What's the matter Alan, we're still in with a shout, aren't we?' But it wasn't the game or the result which was bothering him and he replied: 'I've just heard a rumour that Jim Smith is going to sell you. It's nothing definite, mind.' I thought to myself, 'They won't sell me, I've only just got here', but Alan wasn't so sure and he promised to ring me the next day if he heard anything more concrete.

CHAPTER TEN

Blue is the Colour

As soon as I got home after the Watford game I sat down and thought about what Alan Oliver had said about Newcastle supposedly wanting to sell me, but it still didn't make any sense. Time and time again I tossed the idea over and over in my mind and on each occasion came up with the same conclusion – why should Jim Smith want to sell me? I didn't want to believe my Newcastle career was over but the more I thought about the events which transpired at Watford the more I began to think that Jim did want me out. For a start, I did see Jim talking to Bobby Campbell and later in the night the boss, knowing that I was staying down in London to record a TV programme called *You Bet* with Bruce Forsyth, had asked me to give him a telephone number where he could contact me if necessary. At the time it didn't occur to me that something was cooking and it wasn't until the next morning when I got a phone call from Bobby Campbell that everything started to fit into place. Jim Smith wasn't after Dixon or Durie at all, he was selling me. Mr Campbell said that he'd spoken to Jim and received permission to talk to me.

I couldn't believe that Jim hadn't had the decency to tell me about it and that I should discover from the manager of

Chelsea that I was no longer wanted at Newcastle. To begin with I was lost for words but as everything began to sink in I thought to myself, 'If Jim doesn't want me, why shouldn't I talk to Chelsea?' I agreed to meet with Bobby Campbell to discuss a possible move but I was still annoyed with the way things had been handled on Newcastle's part. I found out later that even before I'd received that call from Bobby Campbell stories were being put out on local radio on Tyneside that I was having talks with Chelsea that day. The fans back home probably knew about it before I did. What sort of way is that to do business? OK, so Jim needed money to buy new players and realised he could get a few bob for me, but why the hell didn't he bother to tell me about it? After all it was my career they were dealing with. Jim said later that he never wanted to sell me but was forced into it because he knew he could get about £800,000 for me and that he had two other 'capable 'keepers' in Tommy Wright and Gary Kelly at the club. Some time later he told me: 'In an ideal world I wouldn't sell you but I need money to finance others deals.' Suddenly I was an item in an auction.

At the end of it all Jim did wish me all the best but in my mind they were hollow words which I paid little attention to. As far as I was concerned he wanted to sell me and that was it. So while I'd never wanted to leave Newcastle I weighed up the situation and thought to myself, 'What the heck, let's hear what they've got to say.' I was so impressed with Bobby Campbell that I agreed to join Chelsea there and then. I couldn't sign until I'd passed a medical the following day but that was never going to be a problem and a Press conference was arranged to announce my signing.

That was when we hit a snag. Because Newcastle still owed Wimbledon money for me, they wanted more cash up front from Chelsea to enable them to pay off the debt. Newcastle wanted an extra £50,000 on the table but Chelsea wouldn't agree to that and for one awful moment it looked as though the deal was off – especially when Ken Bates lost his rag and announced: 'If Dave Beasant is not a Chelsea player by five p.m. he will never be a Chelsea player.' So from being a lot at an auction I was now a pawn in a game of chess.

To add to the chaos, right in the middle of the talks, my agent reminded me that I'd got a contract with ITV to record the *You Bet* programme that afternoon. So, with the whole deal precariously balanced on a knife edge, off I went to the studios not knowing which club I would be playing for in two days' time. My mind was in turmoil and I'm surprised I managed to get through the programme without making a complete idiot of myself. There I was, a judge on a TV panel with the cameras rolling, trying to concentrate on what was going on around me but with a million and one things going through my mind. It was a crazy situation to be in and I'll never forget that day as long as I live.

After the show we resumed talks with Bobby Campbell and Ken Bates and, in the early hours of Wednesday morning, all the discussions, the frantic phone calls and the fax messages were over. We had finally come to an agreement – albeit a strange one because in effect I was financing my own transfer. Newcastle still owed me money from my original signing-on fee, to be spread over my five-year contract, but as they wanted to terminate that contract I was well within my rights to expect the cash in a lump sum. The plan was that Chelsea would take over Newcastle's debt to me and my ex-club would knock it off the fee. Complicated or what? I was delighted, not to mention relieved, that both parties were finally in agreement and everything had gone through because by then I was convinced a transfer to Chelsea was the best thing for me. Although the move meant I was dropping down a division I was sure it would only be a temporary thing and that the club would be back in Division One next season. And, with the way things had been going at St James' Park, there was a fair chance that Chelsea would be changing places with Newcastle in a few months' time.

Bobby Campbell impressed me immensely throughout the talks and the thing that probably swung it for me was when he said to me: 'If you don't sign I THINK we will win promotion, if you do sign I KNOW we will get promotion.' That was good enough for me and it was nice to hear, a great boost to the ego after such a disappointing time, in terms of results at least, at Newcastle. Not that my confidence had been affected in the previous months. I was happy in my own mind that Newcastle hadn't sold me because I hadn't performed up to scratch or anything like that. I'd been pleased with the way I'd played for the club and so had the fans. Even though we had made an awful start I had been performing well and in the opening games hardly put a foot wrong – as was proved by the fact I won the season's first Player of the Month award in the North East. Supporters were coming up to me and saying things like 'Thank God for you' and 'Without you we'd be in even bigger trouble', so I couldn't have been doing that badly. It wasn't as if they were questioning the club's decision to spend so much money on me and, judging by the mail I received after I was sold to Chelsea, they were sorry to see me go.

Just to set the record straight, I never wanted to leave Newcastle and at no time did I ask for a transfer, but what option did I have? The club had had problems all season and Jim Smith clearly thought he needed to buy Newcastle out of trouble. To do that he needed to raise cash and that's where I came in. It was a sad end to my career on Tyneside because I expected so much of my record-breaking move but I wouldn't have missed going to Newcastle for the world. It was a great experience for me and my family. I loved the people up there and don't regret joining the club for one minute. My only regret was that we didn't do as well on the field as I'd hoped when I left Wimbledon. At the time I packed my bags and headed north for Newcastle I was glad to leave Wimbledon because I needed a new challenge but maybe I didn't realise what a good thing I had going at Plough Lane. Amidst all the troubles and traumas which made my short stay on Tyneside so eventful, to say the least, I must admit I missed the spirit and the atmosphere of the Wimbledon family. They say you don't appreciate things until they are no longer there and I found that to be true.

But, having said all that, I'd gone to Newcastle full of hope and optimism. I'd joined a big club with tremendous poten-tial, a fabulous following and with the new signings the club had made – myself, Andy Thorn, John Robertson and John Hendrie – I was looking forward to chasing the major honours. I had signed a five-year contract which I'd hoped I would see out. Despite the loss of Paul Gascoigne in the summer there was an air of confidence about the place which made you think we were in for a good season. The team looked as though it had everything we needed, a mixture of youth and experience, brawn and brains, flair and reliability. It seemed we couldn't go wrong and even the appalling start we made at Everton was seen as a temporary hiccup. I'm afraid to say the hiccups stayed with us virtually throughout my short stay on Tyneside.

Of course, it wasn't just on the field that the club had problems. Behind the scenes there was always something going on to add to the unrest as time went by. All the talk of a takeover bid by the Magpie Group was new to me but such was the depth of feeling among the fans and the Press about the Newcastle board that it was hard to ignore. On joining Newcastle, I was told to be wary of the board. People warned me of their reputation for selling off their best players because they were more interested in having money than building a winning team. Of course I was aware of the ill-feeling the sale of the likes of Gazza, Chris Waddle and Peter Beardsley had created but to me it seemed as though times had changed. The club had made money available for Willie McFaul to bring in fresh blood and the feeling I got was that Newcastle were on the threshold of a new and hopefully successful era. Little did I know what lay ahead and that, after a management reshuffle, I would be following Gazza and Co out of Newcastle.

The problems began with the sacking of Willie and his number two, John Pickering – a panic measure in my view when you consider that we were less than a third of the way through the season when they were given the boot. Understandably the fans had become frustrated and agitated but it wasn't Willie they wanted out, it was the board. They weren't too critical of him or the team, although they were obviously unhappy with the position the club was in. Throughout it all, Willie handled the situation superbly and tried to keep the pressure off the players by taking any flak that was flying himself. He was happy to be the one who had to keep answering to the Press after every defeat and he always used to tell us:'Don't worry about me, you just get out there and do your stuff.'

The main criticism aimed at Willie was over the absence of a big centre-forward, a larger than life figure the fans could hero-worship – someone like Malcolm 'Supermac' Macdonald or Jackie Milburn. We didn't have a goal-scoring machine with that sort of magnetism or status and that was something which frustrated them more than anything. There was a time when John Fashanu was linked with the club and I feel that, had Willie managed to sign him, he would have fitted the bill – and the coveted number nine shirt – perfectly. Fash has got that sort of charisma, as anyone who knows him will tell you. Unfortunately he also carried a price tag of well over a million pounds and that was enough to kill any interest Newcastle might have had in him.

I also remember fans coming up to me and saying: 'Get your mate Vinny Jones up here.' Incredible really when you think that not so long before, they hated his guts, and yet suddenly he was the type of player they felt the club needed to add a bit of steel. That was certainly something we could have done with at the start of the season when the character and resolve of certain players left a lot to be desired. We were lacking vitamins A and D – aggression and determination – and having come from a team like Wimbledon where everyone fought for each other, it was frustrating to watch.

One thing I felt all along about Newcastle was that we had the skill, but didn't possess the team spirit or the determination which can overcome any flaws you might have. We fought as individuals, not as a team. But, contrary to some reports – especially in the tabloid Press in London – I wasn't unhappy at Newcastle. People suggested I couldn't settle in the North East but that was never the case. After a chat with Willie and the chairman at one point I even went on record in the papers in Newcastle as saying I was happy at the club, which I was.

The only problems were the results on the field because, after all the expectancy and optimism, the season started to turn sour and the pressure on the boss was mounting all the time. I remember walking into the dressing-room after we'd just drawn with Charlton in a League game towards the end of September and looking at Willie's face. We had just conceded a late goal and drawn a game we should have won and he was completely distraught. He must have been thinking 'Somebody up there doesn't like me', and we all felt for him because the Press were ready to hang him there and then. A few days later, when we'd lost to Sheffield United in the Littlewoods Cup, Willie's position was even more desperate and he looked as though he was going to crack at any minute. We were frightened to look him in the face or say anything to him and you could sense then that he was on the way out. And although we won at Liverpool the following weekend, a shock result if ever there was one, the victory was merely delaying the inevitable. The noose was still right around his neck, all it needed was for someone to kick the box away. Sure enough that happened after the very next game when we went down 3-0 at home to Coventry.

Yet while I was half expecting him to get the chop the news, when it came, took me aback and I couldn't help but feel sorry for Willie. As one of the players he had brought to the club in the close season, and as his captain too, I felt responsible for his demise. I was one of the people he'd bought to strengthen the side and, although I believed I'd performed reasonably well, I couldn't help thinking I'd let him down. The day we were called together at the training ground and Willie came in to tell us he'd got the sack I felt sick. He tried to put on a brave face but you could tell he was completed gutted, demoralised and distressed by the whole experience.

Yet even though he must have been at his lowest ebb he tried to lift the players, assuring them that some good would come of his sacking; that the pressure wouldn't be so great and that we had the ability to come through this without him. If we had been dealing with a manager we didn't particularly respect and who deserved the sack then no one would have batted an eyelid, but Willie was such a genuine, honest man we all liked – at least I did. He deserved better than that. It was the players who had been at the club a long time, those who had worked with Willie down the years, who felt the decision more than most. They were unanimous in the view that the board, under pressure themselves from the fans and the Magpie Group, had taken the easy way out by sacking the manager.

To my surprise the senior players demanded a showdown with chairman Gordon McKeag in the gymnasium, after Willie was sacked, to express our feelings in a vehement manner. Willie had always told us that he didn't like the board and that there was only one genuine person sitting on it. That man, he insisted, was the chairman. Mr McKeag was the one who had taken all the flak but, according to Willie, he was the one good guy among a bad bunch. The chairman explained to us that Willie had been sacked purely because of results on the field. That was when the fun started because some of the lads accused the chairman and his board of 'bottling it', saying that they'd only sacked Willie to take the pressure off themselves. Mr McKeag didn't go along with that, surprise, surprise, and he refused to go back on the board's decision. Other than go on strike there was nothing we could do. Willie was sacked.

A number of the players (myself, Glenn Roeder, John Anderson and Kenny Wharton) went round to his house after training to apologise for his sacking and wish him all the best for the future. I think it had started to hit him by then and he must have been close to tears. As a relative newcomer to the club I felt strange being there with players who had known him, drunk with him and shared the ups and downs with him for years. I felt a bit out of place and awkward but, as captain, felt I should visit him and say something on behalf of the rest of the lads. I just said my piece and left. I told him I was sorry he'd got the boot and that I felt I'd let him down. He assured me I hadn't.

Willie's demise was induced by a range of things, not least the attitude of certain players and lack of commitment when things weren't going well. Maybe that was down to the fact that Willie wasn't hard enough on players who possibly took advantage of his gentle nature and his softly, softly approach to management. There were times when he was too kind for his own good and even he admitted that, had he taken a hard line during his time in charge, he would probably still be there now. Just one example of his generous nature was the way he would allow Londoners in the side, people like me and Thorny, to go back home a couple of days before a game in the capital. We would travel down on the Thursday while the other players would train on Friday morning and meet up with us at a hotel in the evening. We would also be allowed to stay down in London after the game rather than travel back to Newcastle with the rest of the squad. It was a typically kind gesture on his part and one we appreciated but I wonder how many managers would have been prepared to let that happen. Looking back, you would have to say that things like that didn't exactly encourage team spirit or unite players as a squad.

I said all along that, while the team wasn't short of skilful, gifted individuals, we lacked togetherness and passion. At Newcastle we played as individuals whereas at Wimbledon we had always fought as a unit and by doing so overcame weaknesses elsewhere in our make-up. Newcastle's weakness was that it was every man for himself and we rarely pulled together for the same cause. On the occasions we did play as a team we looked good and capable of holding our own against anyone.

It would be easy to point the finger at the manager for not generating team spirit and togetherness amongst his players but at the end of the day he can only do so much. Once you cross the touchline it's down to the player himself to carry out his job professionally and with the utmost regard for his team-mates. On too many occasions there would be warring factions among the squad; the defence blaming the forwards for not scoring and the strikers blaming the back four for not preventing the opposition from scoring. It was crazy. I have always preached that you start attacking in defence and you start defending in attack. If you prevent the opposition crossing the half-way line they are not going to score, it's as simple as that. Unfortunately, we never operated that way and basically that boils down to a lack of discipline among players who are not doing the job to the best of their ability.

I found it incredible that, in the first game we played after Willie was sacked, we went out with the attitude, 'Let's win this one for Willie'. Why the hell we didn't take that standpoint when he was in charge I'll never know. Had we done so he might still be the manager of Newcastle today. But despite all the problems, the frustration of being in a struggling side only got the better of me once – after the 4-0 defeat at Millwall – when, in a moment of madness, it crossed my mind to leave Newcastle. I never carried out my threat though. I had signed for five years and, as far as I was concerned, I would be at St James' Park for that length of time . . . and possibly more. And throughout it all I can honestly say that my self-belief and confidence in my ability as a goalkeeper never wavered once. I had always given 100 per cent and, even faced with the bitter disappointment of Willie being shown the door, I was determined to give the new boss, Colin Suggett, total commitment.

Within a week of Willie's sacking all the big names in football management were linked with Newcastle. Arthur Cox, Howard Kendall, Lawrie McMenemy; you name them, we were after them and it was heartening to know that the board was thinking big. That's why we were so surprised when the club originally named Suggy as manager rather than caretaker boss because the word was that he was only keeping the seat warm for Howard Kendall.

I got on well with Suggy in my short time at the club and found him a nice, easy-going bloke but it was obvious to me that some of the longer-serving players had serious doubts about his qualities as a manager. The general feeling amongst the squad following his appointment was of disappointment and concern. Although Suggy had been assistant manager at one stage he was apparently moved back down to youth team coach and replaced by John Pickering. The lads claimed that training was boring with Suggy running the show and that they couldn't respond to his methods. They were worried that the same thing would happen again with him in command and the question they were all asking was, 'What's the club coming to?' It wasn't for me to comment on Suggy's shortcomings as a manager but the players who had been at Newcastle for some time couldn't understand how a man who couldn't handle the assistant manager's job should suddenly be put in charge.

I didn't know what had gone on at the club in the past or what sort of relationship Suggy had had with the players but it seemed to me that a lot of the lads had lost respect for him. They had been waiting for a major appointment and when it didn't happen the senior players were again left to question the aspirations of a board of directors which had long been accused of lacking ambition. They had sold their best players and then replaced Willie with the youth team coach. To most people at the club that was a backward step.

It wasn't difficult, even for an outsider like me, to sense the despondency within the club at that time and morale was very low. Training was no longer fun and you would go into work to find players moaning about this, that and the other. Inevitably that disillusionment spilled over into games and into the dressing-room on match days. There were bust-ups after games we had lost, with players having a go at each other and Suggy caught up in the middle, powerless to quell the growing unrest. We exchanged words when Willie was in charge but he would always step in to prevent things getting out of hand. That wasn't happening with Suggy at the helm. It got to the stage where players were literally at each other's throats and needed to be separated by the other lads. That was the sad state of affairs we had reached and suddenly playing for Newcastle wasn't enjoyable any more. Until that time (around Christmas) the atmosphere hadn't been too bad and, despite all the problems we'd had on the field, the spirit among the players had been reasonably sound. But with results continuing to go against us the mood in the camp became more tense and the squad was split.

The thing that surprised me most was the little cliques which existed within the club; players who lived in the same area of town or players who had grown up together at the club. I found it hard to understand that they would gather in their little groups and have a moan about 'the other lot over there' and vice versa. There also seemed to be a division between players who had been at the club a long time and those like me who were relative newcomers – and Kenny Wharton added fuel to the fire with an outburst in the Press. Kenny argued that, while people assumed professional footballers to be highly paid with big houses and flash, sponsored cars, he had been at Newcastle for ten years but still lived in a three-bedroomed semi and drove a five-year-old car. I felt that his comments were aimed at people like me and, rightly or wrongly, I took them to heart somewhat. Maybe I was over-reacting or being over-sensitive but at the time I felt his comments were unnecessary. My argument was, and still is, that part of the lure of joining a new club is getting a sponsored car and being well-paid. I had done my time in the lower divisions playing for one of the smaller clubs and now it was my turn to be overpaid and well looked after.

A few of the lads took his accusations the wrong way and inevitably it added to the ill-feeling gushing through the club. I could understand Kenny's feelings to a certain extent because, having been at Wimbledon a long time, stories of players earning more than me were unsettling. But the thing to remember is that you have signed a contract and you have to abide by it.

As Newcastle skipper I considered it partly my responsibility to sort out problems of this nature but, being relatively new to the club, it placed me in an awkward position. Unlike the situation I was in at Wimbledon where I knew everyone inside out, knew what made people tick and therefore knew how to handle them, I couldn't identify so readily with certain individuals at Newcastle. At Wimbledon if there were any problems or misunderstandings we would always go out for a meal and a few drinks to sort things out. That didn't happen at Newcastle, not until the day we lost 3-0 at home to Coventry, that is.

We had quite an enjoyable night out trying to put the world to rights and, despite losing 3-0 at home, the fans we bumped into weren't too hard on us. I remember talking to my old Wimbledon mate Glyn Hodges about his brief spell at Newcastle and he warned me, 'If you lose at home, don't go

out. If you win, go out and fans will buy you drinks all night.'
But I didn't sense any animosity towards the players and I will
always have the greatest respect for the Newcastle supporters.
As for the night out itself, it didn't produce the benefits I'd
hoped because by the Monday morning, just two days later,
Willie was sacked and everything we'd discussed was instantly
forgotten.

If anything things got even worse after that and St James'
Park wasn't the happiest place in the world to be at that stage.
Personally, I felt I got on well with the majority of the players
and on a one-to-one basis there were no problems as far as I
could see. But I never knew what these people were like when
they were back in their little cliques, or what they were saying
behind my back.

The only real rows I had during my time there, however,
were with management; one with John Pickering, one with
his first replacement Mick Martin and the other with Colin
Suggett. The argument with Mick came about after the 4-0
defeat at Millwall when he blamed me for a deflected goal I
could do nothing about. I was so incensed that, in the heat
of the moment, I turned round and told him to find another
'keeper if the club wasn't happy with me. I don't normally lose
my cool but on that occasion I did and afterwards I regretted
the stupid things I'd said. To make matters worse the incident
occurred at a time when Spurs were rumoured to be interested
in me and were supposedly preparing to make a £1 million
bid.

Prior to the game at The Den I had warned Suggy that
I would be staying in London over the weekend as I was
attending an awards presentation on the Monday organised by
Panasonic and therefore would miss the first training session of
the week. It wasn't until I reported for training on the Tuesday
and I spoke to Andy Thorn that I learned I was in hot water
with the boss. Thorny told me that Suggy had been going up
the wall because I wasn't in training on the Monday when an
inquest had been held into the defeat at Millwall. It wasn't
long afterwards that Suggy pulled me about it and demanded
to know where I'd been the previous day. I explained to him

that I'd been at the Panasonic awards and he looked at me as if to say, 'Are you sure?' I told him that I'd cleared it with the club and I reminded him of the conversation we'd had about it. But because of all the rumours about me and Spurs he was convinced I'd been at White Hart Lane having talks with Terry Venables. I assured him I'd been at the awards' ceremony and nowhere else but he still insisted on seeing me in his office after training.

It was a bit like the Spanish inquisition and it was obvious he didn't believe my story. When I saw him later he asked me if I'd got the hump with Newcastle and if I was looking to get away, saying that he'd heard all the stories that Spurs were interested in me. He seemed convinced that I didn't want to play for him, didn't want to play for Newcastle but, despite all that had happened, I went to great lengths to confirm I wasn't after a transfer.

As for the ruck I had with John Pickering that came a lot earlier and was much ado about nothing but typical of the type of atmosphere which had built up at the club. He had a go at me at one point, claiming I didn't come for enough crosses. He felt I should be putting myself about more and so I had a pop back at him saying something like:'It's easy for you to criticise when you are sitting on the bench or watching a video. It's a whole new ball game when you are out there and you have to make a spur of the moment decision.' Once I'd expressed my opinion he was more inclined to see things from my point of view and, as was the case later with Suggy, the confrontation enabled us to clear the air.

Unfortunately there weren't enough of those sort of exchanges between individuals with the result that problems or gripes people had were not aired. Instead they festered and grew. It would never have happened at Wimbledon where it became something of a standing joke that we would call a 'crisis meeting' to cure the slightest hiccup. We'd even call a meeting to discuss why we hadn't had a meeting for a while! It was a simple procedure, but so effective and if we'd have done the same sort of thing at Newcastle there wouldn't have been such a strained atmosphere within the club. Players were doing their talking but they were doing it in their own little groups and not together as a team with the result that individuals were constantly having a go at each other without the accused person being able to defend himself.

Paul Stephenson was one player who came in for a lot of stick from some of the lads and he must have been upset by some of the taunts of 'Greedy' and 'Thicko' which were commonplace before he packed his bags and went off to Millwall. I'm convinced that it was the attitude of some of his former colleagues which prompted him to leave the club and make a new life in London.

I found it difficult to come to terms with what was going on behind the scenes at Newcastle and said all along that what we needed at St James' Park was a touch of the Wimbledon spirit. I even had Newcastle fans coming up to me and saying exactly the same thing. I remember saying to somebody that if you put Wimbledon in Black and White stripes and they won every week you would get 40,000 coming through the turnstiles every home match, no problem. They love their football in the North East but winning is all that matters and they don't care how you do it. They just wanted success and we hadn't given it to them.

The ironic thing about Suggy's sacking was that, for all his faults as a manager, we had just started to get it together as a team when he was axed and Jim Smith was appointed in his place. Having originally thought Suggy wasn't the right man for the job, he'd begun to turn things around and his reward was the sack. It didn't seem fair and you couldn't help but feel sorry for the man. Suddenly from being boss he was back in charge of the youth team and it seemed strange to see him doing odd jobs around the place; collecting bibs in training or clearing up the cups on match days.

Nobody really knew too much about Jim Smith as a person or as a manager but it didn't take us long to realise he was a man of great character and strong principles. On his first day in charge he called us all together to lay down his rules. He opened up by saying that while players might call him all the names under the sun behind his back, to his face we must refer to him as 'boss' or 'gaffer'. It may only have seemed a small matter of principle but it left us in no doubt that he was in charge and that we would be doing things his way.

He explained how important it was to put the club back on the map and almost immediately he gave the place a lift. Together with his assistant Bobby Saxton, a bubbly, enthusiastic character, he instilled a new atmosphere and his arrival was literally like a breath of fresh air. He introduced different ideas into what had become predictable training methods and virtually overnight work was fun again. People were laughing and joking after training, the boss included, and even before we'd kicked a ball competitively under Jim Smith we got the feeling we were on the way back.

The atmosphere at the club and the attitude of the players was completely different to when Suggy took over from Willie. Everyone knew Suggy and he knew them and players didn't feel they had to go out and impress him, but with Jim at the helm everyone was buzzing and desperate to show him they were worthy of a place in his team. Even in training players were throwing themselves into tackles and putting themselves about as if their whole careers depended on it. I remember thinking at the time that if we could transfer that attitude and commitment to the field of play on a Saturday afternoon we would be out of trouble in no time.

When we won our first game under Jim Smith – against my old club Wimbledon – he was instantly hailed a 'Messiah' and there was a new sense of optimism and excitement on and off the field. Before that first game the boss called me into his office and, like Willie and Suggy before him, was keen to know if I was as unsettled at the club as certain newspapers had made out. He said that he'd read in the Press down in London stories that I was unhappy and looking for a move down south and he wanted me to level with him. I simply told him what I'd told the previous two managers – I was happy at Newcastle. He said that was the news he'd wanted to hear and I thought no more of it. You can imagine my surprise then when he sold me almost a month to the day after telling me what an important part I had to play in the club's future.

Three days before I was sold to Chelsea, Jim relieved me of my duties as captain and although I can understand an outsider thinking that had a bearing on my transfer, it wasn't the case. It was, however, a disappointing end to my Newcastle career. But there's no time for regrets in football and no time for looking back – especially as I was to make my Chelsea debut 48 hours after signing for the London club. I didn't have a lot of time to prepare for my debut but I felt confident I wouldn't let the club down. Having fought long and hard to get into the First Division with Wimbledon, I wasn't exactly overjoyed about the prospect of going back down to the Second. But I was convinced it would only be for half a season.

CHAPTER ELEVEN

The Road Back: A Chelsea Diary

Saturday, 14 January 1989 Chelsea 1, Crystal Palace 0

My debut for Chelsea and by no means an easy baptism. The club had lost their last two games – against Barnsley in the FA Cup and Nottingham Forest in the Simod – and conceded eight goals in the process, so we were under a bit of pressure. We were still top of the Second Division but the onus was definitely on me to keep a clean sheet in front of a big home crowd in excess of 24,000. Although I'm what you might call an 'experienced campaigner' I was a little tense before the game but the pressure of playing for a team going strong and chasing promotion is a damn sight nicer than that I'd been experiencing in a struggling side at Newcastle. I could tell the lads were full of confidence, something I hadn't sensed for some time, and the reception the Chelsea fans gave me soon put me at ease and in a similar frame of mind. Even before the game kicked off I had a feeling it was going to be my day. Thankfully I was right and the match could hardly have gone better. I struck up a good understanding with my back four almost instantly and there were few moments of danger to contend with early on. The team didn't play particularly well, though, and after Tony Dorigo had put us in front just before half-time we were happy to hang on.

From a personal point of view I was delighted to have produced the goods on such an important day and the praise heaped on me afterwards was very heartening. The papers were very kind too, suggesting I was a snip at £750,000 and while that might be stretching the point it was certainly the best start I've made for a club. In my first game for Wimbledon I let a goal through my legs and for Newcastle I was picking the ball out of the net just 34 seconds into my debut at Everton, so I couldn't be happier.

Saturday, 21 January 1989   Blackburn 1, Chelsea 1

Our preparations for what was always going to be a tough visit to Ewood Park were far from ideal . . . to say the least. At two-thirty a.m. (yes, a.m.) the night before I was awoken by Chelsea phsysio Bob Ward and needless to say there were a few choice words flying around my bedroom as I replied to his hammering on my door at such an ungodly hour. I can't remember my exact words but 'What the **** do you want?' was the essence of it. I was told to get my track suit on and join the other lads down in the lobby because there had been a bomb scare in the hotel. A taxi driver had apparenly ear-wigged a conversation involving an Irishman he'd picked up and he claimed he heard him say: 'After what happens at four a.m. there will only be one team at Ewood Park tomorrow.' It all sounded very dramatic and the hotel was evacuated in case a bomb did go off at four o'clock. We all piled on to the team coach at about three-thirty and sat there for an hour waiting for the big bang which never materialised. The police searched the hotel and were happy it was a hoax and we were allowed back to bed.

If the idea was to disrupt our preparations then it worked but it was Blackburn who looked half-asleep as Kerry Dixon fired us into a seventh-minute lead. I was called on to make a couple of saves and although we were 1-0 up for an hour I could sense we were going to get punished for sitting back on the lead. Sure enough, with about 15 minutes to go, Blackburn equalised following an in-swinging corner and we had to settle for a point.

Saturday, 4 February 1989   Walsall 0, Chelsea 7

With Walsall struggling at the foot of the division we fancied our chances of turning them over – despite losing Tony Dorigo with a stomach bug just before the game. But never in our wildest dreams could we have imagined we'd hit them for seven. Playing against a big club like Chelsea we expected Walsall to raise their game, just as Wimbledon always did against the likes of Liverpool or Manchester United, and Bobby Campbell's pre-match message was one of warning not to take Walsall lightly. I remember him saying: 'This will be the best Walsall have played this season.' Nice one, boss. Afterwards we walked into the dressing-room and joked with him: 'If that's their best, we'd hate to see their worst.'

Although Kerry Dixon was missing, Gordon Durie and Mickey Hazard were back on first-team duty and it was the combination of the two that destroyed Walsall. It was from Mickey's corner that 'Juke Box' put us ahead early on and after 22 minutes Gordon had completed a brilliant hat-trick. After his first goal Walsall had a chance to score, but I managed to pull off a save and that was probably the turning point. Had they got back on level terms it could have been a different story, but almost straightaway Gordon made it 2-0 and they were beaten. Although we went in 4-0 up at half-time (Kevin Wilson scoring the fourth) the boss gave us a ticking off because we had started to get a bit cocky and errors were creeping into our play. He warned us against complacency and urged us to finish the match off in a professional manner. Two more goals by Gordon and a penalty by Graham Roberts in the second half seemed to satisfy him. We'd stuck to our task well. Gordon showed what a quality striker he is with some superb finishing and I can't help wondering what the score might have been had Kerry been playing. I'd hardly had a stop to make but succeeded in saving a Stuart Rimmer penalty to keep another clean sheet, my second in three games.

Saturday, 11 February 1989   Chelsea 3, Swindon 2

After the 7-0 drubbing of Walsall we were naturally brimming with confidence and when 'Juke Box' put us ahead after five minutes another rout was on the cards. We went 2-0 up courtesy of an own goal after 11 minutes and we were coasting, but complacency caught up with us and within a minute they were back in with a shout. Their goal came about as a result of a mix-up between me and Joe McLaughlin but although the goal was credited to Joe, his header, aimed for me, went in off a Swindon player. When we went 3-1 up after 36 minutes through a second Swindon own goal the game was in danger of becoming a mockery. They reduced the deficit (with a normal goal this time) just before the break and the boss was not a happy man at the interval. He had a go at me for the first goal, a bit unfairly I thought, and he was far from impressed with the way we twice squandered two-goal leads. But at least we hung on to win 3-2 and things are looking good for us at the top of the division.

Saturday, 18 February 1989   Plymouth 0, Chelsea 1

The weekend began disastrously for me because no sooner had we arrived in Plymouth than I received a phone call from Sandra saying that the shirt I'd packed to wear to the game was still sitting on our front lawn. I hadn't zipped up my hold-all properly and the damn thing had fallen out of the bag without me knowing, so instead of having a lie-in I ended up spending the morning of the match walking around town looking for another shirt.

I got back to the hotel in time to hear Bob Wilson on *Football Focus* harping on about an incident in my last game for

Newcastle when I was ruled to have handled outside the box whilst taking a goal-kick against Watford. Because Watford scored from the first-minute free kick awarded as a result Bob was making a point of the fact that they must be the only team to have scored with their first kick of the match. Fascinating. Consequently Bobby Campbell told me to be careful with my kicks from now on but, amazingly, I kept getting pulled up for the same thing by a flag-happy linesman. The first time it happened it may have been touch and go but on the second I deliberately stayed well inside my penalty area as I released the ball to kick. Still he penalised me and continued to give everything against us.

To add to our misery Gordon Durie went off just after half-time with a dislocated shoulder. Thankfully a Kerry Dixon goal gave us the points on an awful day down on the south coast.

Saturday, 25 February 1989   Chelsea 2, Oldham 2

There's something not quite right about our performances at Stamford Bridge and again we fell into the trap today of getting on top before allowing our visitors to get back into a game we should have put beyond them. Away from home we tend to take the game to our opponents from the first whistle to the last but for some reason we don't do it at the Bridge. When Graham Roberts shot us into a 2-0 lead after just 23 minutes we looked to be cruising towards an easy win, but by half-time it was 2-1 and we were anything but comfortable. That was how the score stood until three minutes from time when Oldham got a corner and, while most of the defence pushed out to catch them offside, Graham Roberts stayed on the line. When the ball was knocked back in, Roger Palmer was played onside by Robbo and levelled the score at 2-2. Needless to say, the boss wasn't amused because we'd thrown away two valuable points and lost our place at the top of the table. But I'm sure it's only a temporary setback.

Tuesday, 28 February 1989   Chelsea 2, Hull 1

Having returned to London from Newcastle, where every
home game seemed to be played in a Force Ten gale, I was
looking forward to playing in decent conditions again. But
tonight it was Tyneside revisited with a wicked wind blowing all around the wide open spaces of Stamford Bridge. The
conditions certainly weren't conducive to good football and for
45 minutes the fans must have wondered why they'd bothered
to turn up on such a miserable night. The game picked up
in the second half though and within minutes of the re-start
Kerry put us 1-0 up with a powerful header. After 74 minutes,
however, Hull were level – no thanks to me. I must have looked
a right prat as I leapt sky high for a ball which barely bounced
above my knees (you should have heard me explain that one
to the boss). From the rebound Roberts levelled the scores,
but not for long because Kevin Wilson restored our lead two
minutes later. It was by no means a convincing win and so far
in the home games I've played in we've looked anything but
First Division material.

Saturday, 11 March 1989   Chelsea 2, Watford 2

Another home game, another mediocre performance and
another two points dropped. That just about says it all
really. The difference this time, however, was that we were
the ones to come from behind to claim a point. We'd been to
watch Watford at home to Manchester City the previous week
(we didn't have a game because Tony Dorigo and I were both
on England duty in midweek) and although they won 1-0 we
said to ourselves 'We can beat these, no problem.' After just
nine minutes we'd begun to change our tune somewhat with
Paul Wilkinson firing them into the lead as a result of another
defensive mix-up between me and Joe. As a cross came in Joe
thought I was going for it, I thought he would get there and in
the end we were both caught in no-man's-land. In my mind I

made the right decision staying on my line but the trouble with our back four is that, because I'm a big fella, they expect me to come for everything. We've dropped a few clangers like that in recent weeks and it's a bit worrying. Five minutes later we were 2-0 down after good work by my old mate Glyn Hodges encouraged Ewan Roberts to finish with some style. Thankfully Tony Dorigo showed our forwards the way to go with a 25-yard shot over Tony Coton and on the stroke of half-time Graham Roberts put us level with a penalty after Kevin Wilson had been brought down.

It had been a good comeback but it didn't save us from a right rollicking from the boss at half-time. I hadn't had anything to do but had conceded two goals and it was frustrating to feel that I hadn't contributed anything to the game. We could have won the match in the second half but had to settle for a point.

Wednesday, 15 March 1989   Brighton 0, Chelsea 1

Having had a dodgy time of late I was relieved to make a few important saves in the first half as Brighton put us under a good deal of pressure. They didn't do the confidence any harm at all and, although we went in at half-time 1-0 up thanks to a Kevin Wilson strike, the boss wasn't happy. He said:'It's only Beasant who's keeping us in the game.' It was nice to be on the receiving end of some praise again even if it was an indication of how badly we were playing as a team.

The second half wasn't much better and I needed the help of a post to keep them out at one point. In the last minute I made sure of the points with a flying save to deny Larry May, so I left the field a happy man and feeling more a part of the team than before. That was my best performance for Chelsea and I was rewarded for my efforts by being voted 'Man of the Match' by the Brighton sponsors. From the team's point of view, however, this win was nothing to rave about and we will have to raise our game dramatically for our top-of-the-table clash against Manchester City on Saturday.

Saturday, 18 March 1989   Manchester City 2, Chelsea 3

The game had been built up in the Press all week as a Second Division 'Clash of the Titans' and we knew that City's young side – reckoned to be the most exciting in the division – would provide us with THE acid test. With a 40,000 crowd packed into Maine Road, along with the TV cameras, we weren't short of incentives to prove that we were the best team outside the top flight.

We got off to a great start when Kerry put us ahead after 15 minutes following an error by Andy Dibble, who claimed he was fouled going up for a corner. Obviously he didn't realise it was his own man who clashed with him. After 24 minutes Kevin Wilson made it 2-0 and we were cruising, wondering what all the hype about this 'great City side' was about. In fairness they did start to put us under pressure in the second half, but I hardly had a save to make. When Tony Dorigo stretched our lead still further after 70 minutes with a brilliant solo goal we were home and dry . . . at least we thought we were. A dubious penalty gave them hope with just over ten minutes to go and then in the 89th minute we had a scare when we gifted them a silly goal. Little wonder the boss had a go at us afterwards, saying: 'What the hell were you playing at?' He was right to criticise us because you can't go giving away stupid goals even if you are 3-1 up with a minute to go.

Tuesday, 21 March 1989   Sunderland 1, Chelsea 2

Our third away game on the trot and our third victory – that's almost as many as I won in six months at Newcastle! It was nice to go back to the North East, however, albeit to face the inevitable stick from the Sunderland fans and chants of 'Geordie reject'. Before the game I was surprised, but very flattered, to see that a few Newcastle fans had turned up, not to watch the game, but to talk to me and get my autograph. It was a terrific gesture on their part and was indicative of the sort of relationship I had with the superb Newcastle supporters. I'm glad they still think a lot of me and appreciate I didn't turn my back on them.

The game went pretty well too, especially as Graham Roberts put us 1-0 after just five minutes. Marco Gabbiadini looked dangerous for them and while I kept his first effort of the game out I couldn't stop his second – a fierce shot into the top corner. Robbo then had a penalty saved by Tony Norman and the miss really got to him because he was walking around shaking his head for fully five minutes afterwards. The famous Roker roar started to increase in volume as Sunderland pushed forward in the second half, the German lad Hauser bringing a couple of saves out of me. But Kevin Wilson silenced the crowd and gave us all three points when he scored after an hour. The 3,000 Chelsea fans who made the trip to Sunderland were suddenly out-singing the home supporters and they taunted them with cries of 'Where's your famous Roker roar?' They're unbelievable. Afterwards the boss admitted that he'd have settled for five points from the last three away games so he's naturally delighted we're going back to London with all nine. Surely no one can stop us now.

Saturday, 25 March 1989   Chelsea 2, Bournemouth 0

Although Bournemouth had given Manchester United a scare in the FA Cup and were therefore likely to pose something of a threat, we were still on a high after our run of away wins. But if ever there was a case of 'after the Lord Mayor's show' this was it because we were diabolical. We didn't string any passes together and in the first half at least, we didn't create a single chance of note. Not to put too fine a point on it, the football was crap and the rocket we got from the boss at half-time was no more than we deserved. It certainly had the desired effect because after the interval we couldn't stop creating chances. It wasn't until the 68th minute, however, that Gordon Durie made the all-important breakthrough and you could almost hear a huge sigh of relief spread throughout the team. When Graham Roberts made it 2-0 from the spot with ten minutes to go the points were as good as in the bag, but to make sure we decided to 'shut up shop', as they say, and concentrated on keeping things tight at the back rather than going in search of a third goal.

Tuesday, 28 March 1989   Ipswich 0, Chelsea 1

Faced with such a tough encounter against a team also chasing promotion you wouldn't have thought we needed any incentive to raise our game. Although the hard, bobbly pitch didn't make life easy there was no excuse for us having what can only be described as the wrong attitude. Ipswich wanted to be first to every ball and we didn't, with the result that in the opening period I was called on to make a couple of saves from their two dangerous black lads Atkinson and Kiwomya. It was a similar story in the second half with Ipswich reacting quicker than us and picking up most of the loose balls. We hardly created a worthwhile chance for 80 minutes and at one point only Joe McLaughlin's nether regions stood between us and defeat. Good job he's a big lad! But just when the game seemed to be heading for a goalless draw Gordon Durie created something out of nothing and managed to squeeze a shot under Ron Fearon's body with about eight minutes to go. We hung on for another vital win (that's 24 League games unbeaten) but I know as well as anyone at Portman Road that we didn't deserve it. Looking on the positive side though, we did defend well and it's always a good sign when you play badly and still pick up three points.

Saturday, 1 April 1989   Chelsea 5, Barnsley 3

April Fool's Day it may have been, but to concede three goals at home – and still win by two – was almost beyond a joke. It must have been a good game for the fans though, quite literally end-to-end stuff, and it was a personal triumph for Kerry Dixon who hit four. He's getting back to his England best now which is good for him and Chelsea and he is obviously hungry for another crack at the First Division. He came preciously close to leaving the club before my time and, by all accounts, was bitterly disappointed when a move to Arsenal broke down. But, thank God, his future lies at Stamford Bridge. Kerry and Gordon Durie have struck up a terrific understanding and they must be the most lethal duo outside the top flight.

But, while he's always likely to score goals at the moment, there are times when Kerry can be an infuriating player to have in your side. When the ball's at his feet and he's got the goal in his sight there's no hungrier striker around but we are always having a go at him for being such a lazy so and so. The joke is that he stands on a sixpence until a goal-scoring chance rears its head, but ask him to run five yards backwards and he's not interested. Neither will he run for a ball if it's heading towards the corner because he knows there's no hope of him getting a shot at goal. Unless a ball is played straight to him or in front of him he won't budge and he'll look at the provider as if to say: 'It's not where I want it so I'm not running for it.' On one occasion I seem to remember I took a quick goal-kick, punting the ball into a gaping hole for him to run after, and he simply refused to move. I couldn't believe it and more than a few choice words were aimed in his general direction. 'Juke Box' on the other hand is renowned for his unselfish running and he'll chase any cause, lost or otherwise.

But there was no holding Kerry today and he put us ahead after just three minutes before going on to complete his hat-trick in an hour, adding a fourth with about 15 minutes left. Gordon was also on the mark and we ran out comfortable winners . . . in the end. There were one or two question marks against our defence for a time and Joe McLaughlin was disappointed to concede another own goal. It's all happening to him at the moment. Barnsley were 3-2 up just after the interval and it wasn't until the last 30 minutes that we made our superiority tell. Kerry's second goal, our third, was his best and the most surprising thing was that it came from his left foot. The ball boys behind the goal were getting ready to run when he lined up to shoot and we couldn't believe it when we saw the net bulge. Only joking, Kerry.

Tuesday, 4 April, 1989   Chelsea 3, Birmingham 1

With Birmingham rooted firmly to the foot of the Second Division we were expecting an easy match . . . and it showed. For much of the game we looked lethargic, almost disinterested, and afterwards the boss had a subtle dig at us, explaining that we wouldn't have got away with that sort of performance against anyone but the bottom club. He was right but, at the end of the day, we did enough.

They obviously came to the Bridge with the sole intention of keeping the score down and made life toilsome for us by keeping at least eight men behind the ball at all times. We were a goal up at the interval, Kevin Wilson putting us ahead, but bearing in mind that we had conceded a goal against Barnsley within seconds of the re-start the boss told us to guard against a repeat tonight. He said that on Saturday it seemed as though five of us were still in the dressing-room when Barnsley struck. Well tonight I think we must have left six players behind because we allowed Birmingham back into the match a minute into the second half. Typical. Thankfully Graham Roberts restored our lead and Kerry wrapped up the points, but we made hard work of what should have been an easy task. Our approach was wrong and there's a serious danger that complacency is creeping in. That could be fatal at this stage.

Saturday, 8 April 1989   West Brom 2, Chelsea 3

My first ever visit to The Hawthorns and yet another place in the history books – this time as one of an élite band of footballers to have played on every ground in the Football League. In fact I've appeared at 93 grounds if you include Newport.

Albion did their best to spoil my big day and took the lead after just seven minutes when the whole of our defence, myself included, were deceived by a Stacey North throw-in which resembled a corner. He didn't lob the ball high into the box, he fired it in low and hard like a bomb and we were all caught napping as Anderson scored from six yards. Graham Roberts levelled from the spot after Gordon Durie had been brought down and Dave Lee, in for Joe McLaughlin, made it 2-1 after 27 minutes. Then we were caught out by another North throw-in from exactly the same position as the first goal. This time Robbo told me to come for the ball no matter what and I made up my mind to rush off my line as soon as North released the throw. Sounded good in theory, but the trouble was that there were so many players in the box I had to run round them to reach the ball. I could only manage a feeble punch and when the ball dropped on the edge of the area Tony Ford pumped it straight back and I was in no-man's-land. 2-2. We always seemed to have something in reserve though and it was no real surprise when Kevin McAllister made it 3-2 just before half-time. After that it was a case of doing enough to hang on to the points. Had West Brom made it 3-3 I'm confident we would have stepped up a gear and finished them off.

Saturday, 15 April 1989   Leicester 2, Chelsea 0

This should have been a day of great celebration, not just of clinching promotion but setting two Second Division records in the process. Victory would have assured our return to the top flight and extended our unbeaten run to 28. It would also have given us our seventh consecutive away win. That's what should have happened, only Leicester forgot to read the script.

Incredibly there were more Chelsea fans inside Filbert Street than Leicester supporters, about 10,000 making the journey in the hope of witnessing a promotion-winning performance. Before the game the referee came into the dressing-room and explained that the police had warned our players not to run over to our fans should we score or ultimately clinch promotion. They were concerned that we could incite a riot by doing so but, as we pointed out, there was likely to be more trouble if we DIDN'T join in their celebrations. We were adamant that, given a favourable result, we would salute our fans at the end but then a police officer came in and said that if we as much as waved to the fans we'd be in bother. He even threatened to report us to the FA if we disobeyed his instructions and we were all dumbstruck. He was totally out of order but to avoid any hassle we agreed on a compromise whereby we would wave to our fans from the centre circle.

By the time we took to the field a few minutes before three o'clock there were still hundreds of Chelsea fans outside waiting to get in. Police made an announcement requesting the supporters already inside the ground to move forward to make way for their friends. There wasn't really anywhere for them to go, so police and stewards had to start moving kids and parents from the packed terracing into the area which separated our fans from the Leicester followers. The scenes were chaotic and it was somewhat ironic that all this should happen on a day when 95 people were killed at the FA Cup semi-final at Hillsborough. We didn't learn of the tragedy in Sheffield until after the game when our 2-0 defeat suddenly meant nothing.

All in all it was an awful day when everything seemed to go against us. The referee, Mr Fitzharris, hardly gave a single decision in our favour and when he awarded Leicester a dubious penalty big Joe told him: 'You're going to cause a riot if you carry on like this.' Needless to say Joe got booked and I'm sure the ref was getting his own back because we had been reluctant to co-operate when he came in to see us before the match.

Leicester went ahead after 55 minutes when Joe deflected a shot by Paul Reid past me and into the net. At 1-0 I saved a penalty before Kevin McAllister scored what looked a perfectly good equaliser only to have his effort disallowed for offside. How he could be in an offside position when Gordon Durie had pulled the ball back from the by-line heaven only knows. They went 2-0 up after 85 minutes although Nicky Cross was at least five yards offside when he received the ball. Peter Nicholas lost his rag, understandably if you ask me, and was sent off to complete a thoroughly miserable afternoon. We were all feeling low but news of the death toll at

Party time at the Bridge as Dave and his Chelsea team-mates celebrate their return to Division One.

Hillsborough suddenly put the whole thing into perspective. We'd lost a game; 95 people had lost their lives.

Saturday, 22 April 1989   Chelsea 1, Leeds 0

This will go down as one of the strangest days of my career because, although it was a time for celebration as we finally clinched promotion and the title, success seemed so hollow after last week's disaster at Hillsborough. For the past seven days we had all been moved by the pictures from the stadium, the tributes and the flowers but it was only today that it really hit me. I was almost in tears during the minute's silence before the match and as I stood with head bowed I thought to myself, 'It could have been my family, my kids in that crowd.' That was when the full effect of the tragedy dawned on me and I really felt for the people who had lost loved ones. Nine thousand fans from Chelsea and Leeds paid their respects by staying away from the Bridge because what should have been a 39,000 sell-out became a 30,000 crowd as a result of the disaster seven days before.

As a player it was difficult to motivate yourself but with the Second Division Championship at stake we had to turn in a professional performance. Not surprisingly it wasn't a great game and it took a rare strike by John Bumstead after 54 minutes to settle the issue. As the club's longest-serving player it was fitting that he should score the goal which won the Second Division title.

Afterwards I joined in the customary lap of honour but still didn't feel part of the Chelsea set-up. It was a weird feeling because although I had done my bit I couldn't celebrate to the full because I hadn't been involved from the start. I felt I hadn't achieved as much as the other lads and didn't deserve to share the acclaim. I did get into it at one point when we jogged past a huge puddle on the dirt track around the stadium and I turned to Robbo and said: 'Shall we dive in?' With a majestic belly-flop I took the plunge to the delight of the fans. Unfortunately for me I didn't realise that the hole was full of gravel and when I emerged from the water my knees were cut to ribbons, blood pouring down my legs. At least it gave the

Dave crawls out of a puddle with blood pouring from his legs after his party trick went painfully wrong.

fans a laugh, and it didn't cost me £750 which was the price I had to pay for the 'mooning' incident at Plough Lane after Wimbledon won the FA Cup a year ago.

I didn't go out on the town after the 1-0 win over Leeds, preferring to celebrate at home with the wife and kids, but I did go out to a testimonial dinner for Eddie Niedzwiecki the following night. He's a smashing fella and it was a tragedy that his career was brought to a premature end because of injury. Had he still been playing though, I probably wouldn't be going back to Division One with Chelsea. Funny old game, ain't it?

Saturday, 29 April 1989   Shrewsbury 1, Chelsea 1

Our attitude for this game was questionable to say the least, as the boss politely drew to our attention. We'd won the title and Shrewsbury were virtually doomed to relegation so we thought we only had to turn up to win. It took us almost an hour to get going but even when Kerry put us ahead after 55 minutes we didn't take control and we gifted them a point with a goal two minutes from time. After the events of last week this was a real anti-climax and when we got back into the dressing-room everyone was blaming everyone else for what can only be described as an abysmal performance. The defence and midfield were having a go at the forwards for missing so many chances and the forwards were having a go at the others for conceding a late goal. It was a classic case of passing the buck which I hadn't witnessed at Chelsea before. We had always done everything as a team before today but suddenly individuals were bickering and it was silly. We should all take responsibility.

Monday, 1 May 1989   Chelsea 2, Stoke 1

This was another stymied performance and I got the feeling that we'd won the title too early. There was no dangling carrot and we lost the cutting edge we had before clinching the championship against Leeds. At times today Stoke, despite having nothing but pride and self-esteem to play for, made us look complete idiots, playing around us as if we were statues. They looked the promoted side, not us, and took a deserved lead after about 15 minutes when Mark Higgins' downward header bounced over me and I could only push the ball into the roof of the net. Although Kerry levelled just before the break we got a right rollicking from the boss at half-time, justifiably so in my book, and we were warned to show at least some commitment . . . or else. The fans deserved better from the so-called champions. Graham Roberts gave us the points with a late penalty but, as one paper wrote, we were just 'going through the motions'.

At a time when certain ex-Chelsea players, Peter Osgood and Alan Hudson essentially, were giving us some stick in the Press, this performance provided them with more ammunition to have a pop at us. We have not been playing well, it's true, and we are simply adding fuel to their argument that we 'aren't a patch on the great side of the '70s'. They claim we need

A spectacular shot of Dave in action but he couldn't prevent Stoke from scoring at the Bridge on this occasion.

another SIX players if we are to survive in the First Division next season and, on the basis of the last few displays, some might think they have a point. The annoying thing is that the likes of Hudson and Osgood are slagging us off because of what they've seen in recent weeks. They haven't based their judgement on the season as a whole and the form we showed in actually winning the title.

We saw the infamous two in the players' lounge after the game and we wondered what stories they were cooking up for the Press this time. As ex-Chelsea players you'd have thought they would be delighted to see the club back where it belongs. Apparently it was the same old story when Chelsea were last promoted to Division One a few years ago. Their comments have hurt the players and it annoys us to hear ex-pros slagging off their old club for the sake of a few bob. I've got my gun loaded should they continue to slag us off but for the time being, as I'm still a relative new boy, I'm keeping mum. Let's hope they do the same.

Saturday, 6 May 1989   Chelsea 3, Bradford 1

Another typical end-of-season game with neither team having anything to play for, but it was a nice footballing match for the fans to enjoy. Robbo gave us an early lead from the spot, his 12th penalty goal of the season, and although City equalised in the second half Kerry sent the supporters home happy with a brace.

Robbo missed his second penalty of the match but he wasn't upset for long because after the game he was proudly holding the Second Division Championship trophy aloft. Then it was off to a champagne reception at the Houses of Parliament of all places. MP David Mellor is a Chelsea fan and Ken Bates arranged with him for us to visit Westminster. It was certainly a change. Various celebrities were there, including Richard Attenborough and, to our relief, he didn't give one of his Ghandi type speeches. What with drinking champagne on the banks of the Thames and dining out in the Houses of

Heading back to the First Division with Chelsea.

Parliament it was definitely different to the celebrations which followed Wimbledon's FA Cup success last season.

Saturday, 13 May 1989   Portsmouth 2, Chelsea 3

It's common knowledge that we hadn't been playing well of late but we were under orders to put things right today . . . from the chairman, not the manager! Mr Bates came into the dressing-room before the game and, after ushering Mr Campbell out, he told us in no uncertain terms, 'You've got to win this for the boss.' He went on to explain: 'Bobby used to be in charge here and undeservedly was given the sack, so go out and do it for him.' The boss himself hadn't made a fuss about going back to the club which had given him the elbow but the chairman made us realise that a victory was the only acceptable result today. Thankfully we managed to provide the win he so badly wanted although, at the end of the day, it was close.

There was quite a carnival atmosphere at the game with the 'Panda for Peace' DJ Bear doing unmentionable things to an inflatable 'Wicked Willie', the saucy cartoon character. Robbo added to the fun, for the Pompey fans at least, when he scored one of the most spectacular own goals of the season – a bullet-like header into the top corner. I didn't stand a chance. Kevin McAllister got a couple and Clive Wilson made it 3-1 before Mick Quinn pulled one back from the spot after I'd saved an earlier penalty from Warren Aspinall. That's three penalty saves out of five I've made for Chelsea which isn't a bad ratio. With the season over, and a quite remarkable one at that, there's time for me to reflect on a year which has had more ups and downs than a ride on the big dipper.

CHAPTER TWELVE

The Way Ahead

When I pulled on an England jersey and marched proudly out to represent my country for the first time on 16 May 1989 it completed the most remarkable year of my life. In the 12 months which preceded by debut appearance for England – in a 'B' squad match against Switzerland – I had been through more than most players experience in a career. It began on that glorious afternoon of 14 May 1988 when I led Wimbledon to FA Cup triumph over Liverpool, setting three records along the way as the first 'keeper to lead a team out at Wembley for an FA Cup final; the first to receive the trophy; and the first to save a penalty on such an occasion. Within a few weeks of the final I had re-written the soccer history books again when I joined Newcastle in an £850,000 transfer – a record fee for a British goalkeeper. I also become the most expensive Newcastle player in the club's glorious history. Then, following six difficult yet eventful months, I was on my way to Chelsea in a £750,000 deal which made me my latest club's record signing. It also made me even more popular with the bank manager because, as was the case when I left Wimbledon, I didn't ask to go so therefore I received a slice of the transfer fee. Financially, the two transfers set me up nicely for the future and of course security counts for a lot when you're responsible for a wife and two kids.

Now, after years of earning a reasonable if not a great living at Wimbledon, I'm finding out for myself 'how the other half live' – and enjoying it too. I didn't want to spend the whole of my career looking over the garden fence. I wanted to swap my goldfish pond for a swimming pool. But while it might seem I did 'very nicely thank you' out of the two deals, I actually took a cut in wages to team up with Chelsea in the Second Division. So it wasn't just about money. The fact is I didn't ask to leave Newcastle, but the club – or should I say the manager – didn't want me and Chelsea did. The most important thing now is that I'm back in the big time with, potentially, one of the most glamorous clubs in the country. If the plans for the club are as big as those being laid for the redevelopment of Stamford Bridge then a new and exciting chapter is about to be written into the Dave Beasant life story.

Dropping down into the Second Division was something of a gamble and having spent so many years fighting to reach the

Number One ... that's Dave Beasant as he joins in the promotion celebrations with Graham Roberts.

top flight with Wimbledon I didn't give up my place among the greats of English football lightly. I was, however, supremely confident that by the start of the following season I would be back in the First Division. When I joined Chelsea they were in a very strong position at the top of the Second (had they been mid-table with an outside chance of promotion I probably wouldn't have joined) and I was convinced I could help them finish the job off. I would have put money on us winning promotion even at that stage. With Chelsea back where they belong and Newcastle, sadly, doomed to a spell in the Second Division my gamble has paid off . . . with interest.

It was vital to me that I spent no longer than a few months away from the First Division because, having taken a few tentative steps towards international stardom as a Newcastle player, I couldn't afford to be away from the top flight for long. Thankfully I'm back and in a position to press for a full England cap to add to the three I won with the 'B' team in Switzerland, Iceland and Norway in the summer. Before then I had been named in the full England squad and it was a little ironic that I should get a call-up so soon after leaving Wimbledon. Although Andy Thorn had played for the Under-21s, players at Plough Lane rarely got much recognition on an international basis . . . for England at least. Sanch had played for Northern Ireland and Glyn Hodges for Wales but, until Fash made his debut against Chile at the end of the season, no one had been able to catch Bobby Robson's eye. Whether it was down to the fact that Wimbledon have long been soccer's so-called bad boys with a style of play no one seems to like, I don't know.

The Dons' success in the FA Cup final may have altered certain people's opinions and I dare say my personal performance in what was a pressure situation boosted my chances of a call-up more than my move to a big club like Newcastle. When I used to go back to London and talk to the Wimbledon lads during my time with Newcastle some seemed a little aggrieved that I should get my chance having played in a struggling side for a couple of months. Fash, in particular, began to wonder what he had to do to make the breakthrough. Well, now he has

My performance in the Cup final boosted my England chances.

and I'm delighted for him. He got his chance in the Rous Cup games because of injury to Mick Harford and it was a similar situation which led to my inclusion in the England squad for the first time against Sweden last October.

England's three goalkeepers – Peter Shilton, Chris Woods and Dave Seaman – were well-established and seemingly set fair until an injury to Seaman suddenly opened the door for me. The call-up came as a great surprise and it wasn't until a journalist, Rob Shepherd of the *Today* paper, telephoned me at my house in London five or six days before the game that I became aware Bobby Robson wanted me to join up with the squad. Unbeknown to me, Mr Robson had been trying to track me down but even when Rob called to explain the situation I didn't believe him and I remember saying: 'I'll believe it when I hear from the man himself.' Rob then passed my phone number on to Bobby Robson and, sure enough, 20 minutes later I was talking to the England manager who asked me if I would like to join up with the squad. It doesn't take a genius to work out what my reply was. The Russian army wouldn't have kept me away.

*Dave and fellow England 'keeper Dave Seaman dwarf a local Arab
during the national squad's visit to Saudi Arabia.*

At the time it didn't matter to me that I'd got my chance through someone else's misfortune – the important thing was that I'd realised yet another life-long ambition. Even to be considered fourth choice 'keeper for your country is no mean achievement. At least I was there or thereabouts. Because it was my first call-up I asked him what I would need to take to the training camp with me and he said that, in addition to goalkeeping gear, I should take a suit and tie. As I'd left all my decent clothes back in Newcastle I spent the Friday afternoon going round various shops in London looking for a new suit. Being an unusual size that wasn't an easy task because I needed to have the necessary alterations made to the material before joining up with the squad the following morning. When we eventually went to the Sweden game on the Wednesday night I was resplendent in my new suit, shirt, tie and shoes. I looked as if I'd just fallen straight out of Burton's window, a fact which didn't go unnoticed by Gary Lineker who said to me: 'You look smart, Dave, is that a new suit?' Proudly, I said that it was. England mistake number one! Within minutes it was all round the England camp – not to mention the papers next day – that I'd bought a new outfit to mark my call-up. Me and my big mouth.

As it turned out the suit almost didn't make an appearance. For a time there was a chance I would be sporting my England kit as the substitute 'keeper for what was a crucial World Cup qualifier. In the end Chris Woods had recovered sufficiently from his illness to resume his customary role as Shilts' deputy on the bench. I wasn't too disappointed and I simply felt privileged to have spent some time with the squad, training with the country's top two 'keepers. It was a tremendous experience and one which could only stand me in good stead for the future.

I did get on the bench for a friendly in Saudi Arabia but Dave Seaman played the whole game so I was still waiting for my first cap. Again, though, I felt honoured just to be involved and the good thing about it was that because I'd been on the bench in full kit I was allowed to keep my England strip. Anyone can go down their local sports shop and buy an England kit but this was special because I'd earned it and it marked another step towards an international cap. Just being in Saudi was an experience in itself and the stadium in Riyadh was unbelievable, even down to the dressing-rooms which were kitted out with their own gymnasium. The stadium, which seemed to emerge out of the desert almost like a mirage, was absolutely spotless and there were literally people following you around with a dust pan and brush sweeping up behind you.

After the Saudi trip I was left out of the squad which travelled to Greece for another friendly and, while I was disappointed, my exclusion wasn't unexpected. The top three – Shilts, Chris and Dave – were all selected and I could have no qualms about that because none of the lads had done anything wrong to warrant being left out themselves. But I did get another chance to prove my worth, if only in training, when I was recalled to the squad for the World Cup match in Albania after Chris was once again tragically struck down by his mystery illness. I couldn't help but feel sorry for him but it was another great opportunity for me to make another good impression on the England manager. It was hardly what you might describe as 'a glamour trip' abroad but I won't forget the experience in a hurry. From the team's point of view things couldn't have gone better because the lads did a good, professional job under difficult circumstances and came away with two vital World Cup points. The trip was also memorable because it gave me another chance to see at first hand the talents of the man they've labelled the new clown prince of English football – Paul Gascoigne.

Gazza is a one-off and he never ceases to amaze and delight me, both on and off the field. He's forever on the go, forever clowning around and he gets away with murder in the way Wally Downes always did at Wimbledon. The Albanians loved Gazza and he treated them to a solo-show in training which they probably remembered more than the game itself. He had them in stitches with his antics for 20 minutes or more and they cheered him off the training field at the end of it. Afterwards Bobby Robson, who looked to be enjoying Gazza's show as much as the fans, said that Paul had done more for English relations in Albania than any diplomat could do in ten years. He won them over completely.

Gazza was also the star of the show when he scored a superb solo goal at Wembley in the return match against Albania – and he scored with a similarly brilliant effort for the England 'B' team against Switzerland during our summer tour which also took in Iceland and Norway. It was against the Swiss that I collected my first international cap and, although I came off towards the end to give West Brom's Stuart Naylor a run-out, I was delighted to have kept a clean sheet on my debut for my country.

I also came on as a second-half substitute for Stuart in the next match in Iceland and I can honestly say I have never played in such freezing conditions. The wind and rain cut into you so much that your muscles began to seize up and some players even had difficulty moving their arms while running. In the dressing-room at half-time players were visibly shaking from the cold and my Chelsea team-mate Tony Dorigo couldn't even hold his cup of tea. He was throwing it all over himself like a jibbering idiot. Paul Stewart was affected even more by the conditions and he had to come off at half-time because he was suffering from hypothermia. But the game itself was another great success for the 'B' squad because we beat Iceland's first team 2-0 before going on to complete the tour with a 1-0 win in Norway.

Being with the 'B' squad provided me with more valuable experience; it also meant I was continuing to work with Peter Bonetti, the Chelsea and England coach who had already done a lot for me in my short time at Stamford Bridge. Playing in a winning Chelsea side during the second half of the season had put an extra edge on my game after the struggles at Newcastle and, while much of that was down to confidence, a lot was down to the specialist coaching Peter was giving me. Having been used to joining in normal training with the rest of the lads at Wimbledon and Newcastle (doing long distance runs etc) Peter introduced me to a whole new ball game as far as goalkeeper training was concerned. One of the first things he said was that he didn't care whether I was a good long distance runner because he worked goalkeepers in a different way to the norm. I told him I wasn't a bad runner and didn't mind going on runs with the other lads but he preferred to concentrate on other aspects of training, such as agility and positioning. Some of the work he's put me through since I joined Chelsea has been more tiring than anything else I've ever done. After ten years you think you know it all but even some of the basic stuff he has shown me has been different – and difficult too. It was a bit like going back to school, or teaching an old dog new tricks and it took a while for me to adapt, but even after a few weeks of specialist training I began to see the benefits in my game.

Before we started working together Peter said that there wasn't much wrong with my game (which was why Chelsea had paid so much money for me) but he explained that, by working on my agility and the technical side of my game, I could become an even better player. He told me: 'If we can improve you by five per cent then we've done a good job.' Peter has already taught me a lot and working with him on a day-to-day basis can only help me to improve – even at my age.

Without wishing to sound big-headed, I found the Second Division easy from a personal point of view, mainly because Chelsea were by far the best team in the division. Too good in fact. The only difficult game I played for Chelsea last season was my debut against Crystal Palace, and that was tough only because it was my first game for the club and I was under a little bit of pressure to do well and win the fans over early. I succeeded in doing that and from then on I found very little to trouble me during our promotion charge. As was the case with the team as a whole, I considered myself to be above the Second Division and better than everyone else. By winning the title so convincingly we were proved right. We were coasting for much of the season and rarely came up against a team that caused us to go up a gear.

It's a different kettle of fish in the First Division where there are very few easy games but I'm quite an experienced campaigner now and hopefully I can go from strength to strength. I'd like to think I've still got a long career ahead of me and many rivers to cross, and I only have to look at Peter Shilton to see what goalkeepers can achieve even when they pass the 30 mark. By the time he was 32 Shilts had only won 37 England caps. Now look at him, he's 40 and still going strong. I just hope I can emulate him by continuing to play at the top at an age when people expect you to be selling goalkeeping gloves in a shop instead of wearing them. He's a superb pro to look up to and it's been a privilege to train with him and the England squad.

Although my chance for international stardom has come relatively late in my career I'd never given up hope of making it all the way to the top. I'm not there yet but I believe there's a chance and I shall never lose that belief. It won't be easy to break up the trio of 'keepers currently ahead of me in the queue, all I can do is my best. Confidence and ambition are the two main ingredients of a footballer's make-up and I'm not short of either. I've battled my way up from the grass roots right through the divisions to the top flight and I'm justifiably proud of all I've achieved so far. I've had to 'fight for the right'

Dave with the coveted FA Cup. "Hopefully, there will be a few more photos like this to go in the family album."

(as Bobby Campbell says) to be where I am today and I shall continue my fight to go even higher.

The Dave Beasant story doesn't end here. I want to win a Championship medal with Chelsea, a full cap for England and travel to Italy with the World Cup squad. A tall order maybe but, considering all that's happened in my career so far, anything is possible.